# Cambridge Elements ≡

Elements in Reinventing Capitalism
edited by
Arie Y. Lewin
*Duke University, The Fuqua School of Business*
Till Talaulicar
*University of Erfurt, Germany*

# COMPARING CAPITALISMS FOR AN UNKNOWN FUTURE

## *Societal Processes and Transformative Capacity*

Gordon Redding
*King's College London*

Shaftesbury Road, Cambridge CB2 8EA, United Kingdom

One Liberty Plaza, 20th Floor, New York, NY 10006, USA

477 Williamstown Road, Port Melbourne, VIC 3207, Australia

314–321, 3rd Floor, Plot 3, Splendor Forum, Jasola District Centre,
New Delhi – 110025, India

103 Penang Road, #05–06/07, Visioncrest Commercial, Singapore 238467

Cambridge University Press is part of Cambridge University Press & Assessment,
a department of the University of Cambridge.

We share the University's mission to contribute to society through the pursuit of
education, learning and research at the highest international levels of excellence.

www.cambridge.org
Information on this title: www.cambridge.org/9781009303026

DOI: 10.1017/9781009303019

First published 2023

*A catalogue record for this publication is available from the British Library.*

ISBN 978-1-009-30302-6 Paperback
ISSN 2634-8950 (online)
ISSN 2634-8942 (print)

# Comparing Capitalisms for an Unknown Future

## Societal Processes and Transformative Capacity

Elements in Reinventing Capitalism

DOI: 10.1017/9781009303019
First published online: August 2023

Gordon Redding
*King's College London*
Author for correspondence: Gordon Redding, 'gordonredding@cantab.net

**Abstract:** Systems of capitalism are conceived as formed under certain broad logics that apply to all societies, each of which then interprets those logics in distinct ways according to its own processes. Such processes cluster into three categories: an inspiring context, a transformative capacity, and empowered action. The political role is that of balancing the influences across the society at large. Each inspirational influence adds a key contribution, as with benevolent empowering authority and critical thinking. Transformative capacity is built through innovativeness and cooperativeness; and stable decentralized authority flows from communicative action, spontaneous emergent ordering, and competitive productivity. Societal progress may be explained in terms of the integrated workings of these *processes* to yield an ethically legitimate structure for the prosperity-driven creation and distributions of wealth. Two main stereotypes are examined to compare their workings and their outcomes: Western free-market democratic capitalism state-directed forms such as that in China.

Keywords: progress, benevolence, transformation, knowledge, empowerment

ISBNs: 9781009303026 (PB), 9781009303019 (OC)
ISSNs: 2634-8950 (online), 2634-8942 (print)

# Contents

## Introduction

In examining how societies make progress, this Element proposes a form of explanation that differs from many others in current social science; it nevertheless takes its inspiration from respected scholars about understanding and comparing societal complexities.[1] It adopts two perspectives that – although often acknowledged – are rarely applied. These are prioritizing the comparison of *societal processes* alongside institutions and values and assuming a notion of *social pathology* such that societies may be seen in varying conditions of fitness for their pursuit of progress.

The main concepts to be distilled are seen in abstract terms as the universals that all human societies need to exhibit if they are to progress. But these are fluid in nature and in practical interpretation and better understood through narrative description rather than empirical measurement. Their use permits a distinction to be made between the *nomothetic* form of explanation which attempts to identify ultimate causes and the *ideographic* which describes the on-the-ground realities of how such determinants come to be enacted. Working with these two levels of analysis then allows acknowledgement of societal differences in how the universal processes work. These differing enactments of universal principles underlying socio-economic progress can then reveal how such processes have worked better in some societies than others to enable a society's progress. This Element compares the workings in different societies of eight such processes. Societal 'fitness' for progress can then become a consideration to be explained.

Given the theme of societal progress, the central focus is assumed to be people making a living by doing business and consequently building societal resources. The great variety of societal forms is represented in consciously summarizing terms according to two ideal types: the Western form of free-market capitalism and the Chinese system of state-led business. These two overall types are elsewhere expressed in varied interpretations and hybrids and so are to be seen as loosely representative – but still significantly indicative of – fundamental alternative societal philosophies largely shared within each ideal type. For reasons of space, only a brief note will be taken of that further variety, especially the more varied options in the free-market form and in hybrids across the main types.

---

[1] Among those listed in the References, influences include particularly Eisenstadt (1965), Berger and Luckmann (1966), Geertz (1973), Whitley (1999, 2006), Streeck (2012), McCloskey (2016), Bresser-Pereira (2017), Mokyr (2017), DeLong (2022), Galor (2022), Solarino and Buckley (2022), and Neuhouser (2023). Advice from Arie Lewin and Michael Witt is also most gratefully acknowledged, but I confirm that they are not responsible for the interpretations presented.

In recognition of the immense complexity of how societies evolve and interact, it is important to avoid judgemental comparison if it might be taken as blaming policymakers. The 'social pathology' case for objectivity in critique is made by Frederick Neuhouser (2023: 26) in terms which see it at its best when looking forward rather than back; thus: 'the main reason that diagnoses of social pathology do not imply moral culpability is that although the dysfunctions characteristic of them involve failures to realize the good, such failures result from social dynamics, the persistence of which is independent of the intentions of specific individuals; ascribing blame for them to individuals is therefore highly problematic.'

Related to the viewpoint that societies can become dysfunctional is the idea that they carry within them certain functions organized with a 'point' or aim and 'owned' collectively. Such accepted purposes as the China Dream, *noblesse oblige*, or the centrality of freedom go beyond what is possible in non-human biology. The outcome has been that specialized and coordinated activities emerge and stabilize over time, as 'quasi-autonomous *dynamics,* or self-reproducing nexuses of activities that exhibit a characteristic logic or coherence, which means that diagnoses of social pathology rely on a dynamic understanding of social processes, and of how they reproduce and transform themselves over time ... a kind of explanatory holism' (Neuhouser 2023: 346; emphasis in original).

To ensure such objectivity, the position to be adopted here runs parallel to that in the world of medicine. A doctor does not blame a patient but works with a belief in an overall pathology, within which threats to a person's fitness for survival are seen within a set of interacting universal forces that – when out of balance – either can cause specific illnesses or – in advance of that threat – can bring a lower state of fitness. The concluding medical judgements focus essentially on the restoring of bodily equilibrium. An ideal of such balance then unites all the healthcare specialisms and produces a science of pathology that is appreciated for its helpfulness and delivered as informed advice.

So, the medical analogy contains a virtue essential also to social science neutrality, namely it seeks the patterns that determine betterment and working in universally found ways. Neuhouser's fuller reasoning behind this approach builds on the core principle that there are important social phenomena that purely moral or political approaches to social life cannot capture. His main claim is that all of the most respected thinkers on social pathology – including Plato, Hegel, Marx, Nietzsche, Freud, Durkheim, Dewey, and Habermas – have understood reality as *social life*, where the term 'life' is just as important as 'social'. An explanation can, 'without interpretive violence, be made to converge into a general conception of the kind of thing human society is'

(Neuhouser 2023: 346). It gets closer to the reality of psychological, social, and economic patterns of cooperation.

The deeper functional deficiencies that evolve to destabilize societal workings are seen as going beyond the processes applicable to animal – as opposed to human – life, because learning and knowledge are shared in only a very limited way in the animal world. For humans, the knowledge they create and retain becomes arguably the most crucial of all the outcomes from the flow of processes within a well-functioning society (Mokyr 2002; Redding 2023), just as individual wisdom and health consciousness tend to benefit personal well-being and longevity. This means that *societies* can learn in ways far in advance of other complex adaptive systems (other than their *Homo sapiens* components). It also carries the significant assumption, in a changing world, that they need to keep on learning.

Another key explanatory principle derives from the work of Wolfgang Streeck (2012) on societal comparison. This advocates a longitudinal-historical approach focussing on commonalities within national versions of capitalism rather than on their variety. It relies on a separation between the specific *economic* logics that animate capitalist behaviour and the wider *social* logics that apply in any capitalist society, the two perspectives being in constant interplay. Balancing the two while improving a society's shared prosperity is seen as the ultimate political art.

Objectivity must also be grounded in the ultimate facts of geography and history, as any present leadership has no choice but to work with such givens. To illustrate that objectivity for the case of China, the position taken here is that expressed by Oded Galor (2022: 186) in his study of the deepest currents that have shaped human history: 'China has now made the transition to modern growth, in the absence of a major new paradigm shift, and given the scale of the Chinese economy, its geographical connectivity, political centralization, and social cohesiveness, may yet bring China back to the global forefront of prosperity.' The openness of the word 'may' begs the question 'how', and that is what this account attempts to conjecture on the basis of the broad history of *Homo sapiens*.

A further principle derives from the work of Pinker (2016), with his proposition that *all human beings* are born with an inherited set of at least 300 fundamental instincts that guide social conduct wherever they may live. The human mind at birth is not a blank slate, and any attempts to overwrite what is already there will fail if they ignore the deeper instincts that are embedded within all forms of *Homo sapiens*. Such instincts include ways of relating to others socially and hierarchically, as well as instincts to learn and adapt and consequently to survive and flourish as a species for as long as it has so far. Along with aggression, these instincts include the ideals of kindness, compassion, honesty, the need for respect, appreciation of beauty, and coopera-tiveness. Without these, societies stagnate.

So, underlying the variety in how societies work is a deeper layer of human universals which cannot be denied. Reflecting on this, Barbara Tuchman (1962) saw the basic data of history as the human soul – a feature that escapes attempts to imprison it within patterns. It is a consequent contention here that human history shows a tendency for people to avoid mental controls unless they acknowledge a society's version of the human soul. As expressed by the poet Lemn Sissay,[2] who saw the same force as a society's 'heart',

> The spirit of structure can't be foreseen,
> For somewhere between the architecture and the dream,
> More than the sum of the parts,
> Somehow, somewhere, the heart.

Guided by the historian and the poet, this Element asks two ultimate questions of any society: Does it have a human heart? And does it have an inspiring soul? More specifically, it will address the contrast between (1) societies that have released human creativity at very high levels by stabilizing the distribution of influence and (2) societies that have retained central power and have not yet fully released the human creativity within them. To describe societies in a way that clarifies such comparison – and the continuum of blends between the alternatives – is also a way of leaving any society to decide for itself what may or may not be learnt and adopted.

This account is then designed to conjecture that the real answers about how societies make progress are to be found deep in the obscure realm of their people's fundamental instincts. This invisible psychological foundation influences how people live out the universal conditioning of their humanity, whether they are Western, Asian, African, Islamic, Indigenous peoples, city-dwellers, or Pitcairn Islanders. But another basic fact of history lurks in the background: over the last two centuries, the world has changed more profoundly and extensively than in any previous era. In doing so, there has been an explosion in wealth, a rise in risks, and a massive increase in the options and complexities faced by policymakers.

The historical rebalancing of the influences on societal progress, enough to reach this new high level, came about – initially in Europe – through a long-term escape from feudalism. Detailed studies suggest that geography itself fostered the opportunities that were forged by human curiosity (Welzel 2013; Baumard 2016; Frankopan 2023). Eventually the anti-authoritarianism of the Enlightenment became a catalyst for popular movements towards democracy

---

[2] Lemn Sissay was born in poverty in an industrial town in Lancashire to a mother from Ethiopia and brought up in foster homes. He rose to become a respected poet and is currently Chancellor of the University of Manchester.

over the two turbulent centuries of the first major Industrial Revolution. But in Streeck's (2012: 13) judgement, it was not until after 1945 that democratic free-market capitalism became 'a half-way stable political-economic regime in the Western part of the industrialized world, at least for two or three decades'.

The historical picture offered here is derived from a wide literature, but its core themes owe much to the accounts provided by Bresser-Pereira (2017) and by DeLong (2022). These scholars overlap in most of their logics, but they especially agree on two significant themes: the validity of the idea of two fundamental paradigms for economic progress – the state-based *developmental* system and the market-based *liberal* one – each contending for long-term viability, and the idea that after 2010 the world has changed so significantly that a clear 'winner' is no longer fully convincing as a hegemon. At the same time, like Galor (2022), they allow that it is not beyond human learning that a new form might emerge that is able to ward off the threats of poverty and aggression that many see as currently implicit. The two main types now face very deep challenges to the continued viability of their different trajectories.

## A Brief Historical Review

In the summary by Bresser-Pereira (2017), the main sets of institutions that regulate capitalism are those of the state and of the market. Where the state role became dominant, there evolved a developmental class coalition, as was the case in Europe where capitalism began as a government-supported enterprise in its early mercantilist phase. Over the nineteenth century and most of the twentieth, it became liberal, that is, more market-driven. After 1929, more developmental processes were added, based on ideals of democracy and pro-gressivism, but its liberal essence has remained prevalent. Other industrial and capitalist revolutions, as for instance in Japan and South Korea, were shaped under developmentalism, as the state undertook the responsibility for coordin-ating the five most crucial macro-economic prices: rates of profit, interest, wages, inflation, and exchange. The remaining role for the market was then the coordination of efficiency and productivity under real competition.

As noted, Streeck (2012: 5) sees capitalism as inherently unstable and by constant innovation 'permanently revolutionizes the society that it inhabits'. It particularly creates continuing uncertainty in social relations from the tension between its two diverging normative principles: *social justice* vested in the society's 'moral economy' with beliefs about rights and fairness and *market justice* in its 'economic economy', allocating resources by marginal productiv-ity and maximized efficiency, thereby building societal strength. Streeck observes that by the end of the 1960s 'it had become clear that capitalism and democracy [could not] operate side by side without more or less effectively undermining each other' (14). The core political skill became that of inspirationally balancing these tensions as they grow.

To consider the implications of such rising tensions, Bresser-Pereira proposes a semantic widening in the concept of capitalism. Rather than seeing the essential stress as that between socialism and capitalism, he suggests that the alternative to capitalism is more properly a mixed economy – a way not of making capitalism a transition to socialism but instead of making society more efficient and – when it is progressive and social democratic – less unjust. This ideal is a reminder of Heilbroner's (1985) proposition that capitalism had produced a more benevolent form of domination than any prior system. That it would not (yet) be able to make that hybrid work in the face of the then unforeseen complexities met after 2010 is not to disparage the ideal. Thus, Bresser-Pereira's suggested form of developmentalism could evolve as a new variant of capitalism. If so, it opens the possibility of optimism but at the prior cost of much deep thought about its rationale and practical implementation. The essence of such 'new developmentalism' rests on its capacity to meet the principle that 'the more cohesive the nation is, the higher will be the degree of compliance by its citizens with the values and beliefs around which the nation is organized, the more legitimate and capable will be its state, and, so, the lower the level of coercion that will need to be used' (Bresser-Pereira 2017: 683). Alan Murray's (2022) renewed search for the 'soul of business', from his position as CEO of Fortune Media, is an expression of this same concern.

Readers will find echoes of these design principles in the eight processes of this Element's proposed model (Figure 1), to be examined in what follows, with their apex as an 'inspiring context' and with the central role being to balance the total. Using the medical analogy, the design principles of societal cohesion around deep values are the essence of societal 'health' and shape its 'fitness' to face the coming unknowns.

After the Great Depression and the Second World War, Western Europe moved towards a socially progressive form of developmentalism, whereas the United States (and to a lesser degree the United Kingdom) retained its established liberal market capitalism. In Bresser-Pereira's terms, there was an outbreak of unbalanced neoliberalism that brought about the destabilizing Global Financial Crisis in 2008 and the Euro Crisis in 2010. There has been a subsequent tendency for the centre to move tentatively towards a 'conservative developmentalism' but across a wide spectrum of options, its banner now being 'stakeholder capitalism', whereby the focus is on 'linking money to doing good' (Murray and Witney 2022: 195).

Given that capitalism, when seen as a total political/economic response, is taken to be essentially – and perhaps necessarily – unstable, its inherent tensions, and the limits of public policy in trying to manage them, keep

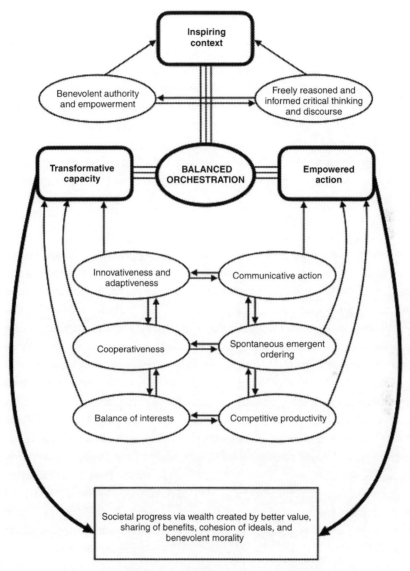

**Figure 1** Vectors of processes in societal transformation.

appearing in a series of world crises. Within living memory, these have included the First World War; the 1930s Depression and the Second World War; the post-war era, most visibly in the 2008/9 crisis; and today the more recent rise in the exploitative dominance of fluid global capital and the new territorial threats coming from Russia and China. States and their economies are separating out between democracies and newly assertive autocracies, with technology and access to technical knowledge and key resources as crucial points of leverage.

Hidden within these trends is the newly identified and universal threat of Artificial Intelligence.

Yet, despite a century of repeated volatility, it must be acknowledged that the free-market democratic form of economy has been resilient (i.e. fit) enough to produce an immense increase in wealth and shared prosperity. Between 1820 and 2016, per capita gross domestic product (GDP) (in 2011 US$) in the United States went from $3,000 to $55,000 and across Western Europe from $2,000 to $42,000. For the 2,000 years before that surge, the world average had long remained at around $1,500 (Koyama and Rubin 2022: 5). Few other responses (other than a late-starting Japan) matched such growth, and most countries now remain clustered around $15,000, with China at a somewhat unclear level estimated by several sources as at $12,000 in 2022.[3]

In a revealing insight about the fundamental differences in approaches between market-driven and state-orchestrated economies, DeLong (2022: 249) explains that in the market-driven case the standard business firm, embedded in its wider economy, works via an endless series of make-or-buy decisions. Can a needed resource be acquired most efficiently inside the firm via managerial forms of social engineering, or is it better to seek budgetary permission to purchase it from outside? Free-market capitalist economies evolve to contain many intermediaries carrying market-related information, and the constant make-or-buy decision-making is enriched by this body of knowledge and the 'crowdsourcing' of policy responses that it stimulates. Rising complexity can thus be absorbed and order incrementally adjusted. A parallel and deeply argued metaphor for this constant flourishing of knowledge exchange in some societies is Habermas's (1984) concept of 'communicative action', whereby widely dispersed reasoning comes to merge with economic decisions. In consequence of such processes, market-driven firms keep themselves efficient and competitively adaptive. In planned economies, this crowd of informed intermediaries has no place, and many business decisions – influenced centrally from a very limited perspective on a narrow base of information – can end up being wasteful.

## The Great Surge

To understand capitalism's resilience today, it is appropriate to identify the societal processes that carried that modern economic miracle and under what circumstances. First, what happened? A momentum had long been building, but it took off from around 1870. Its great prelude was a national gesture of respect towards the combining of knowledge and 'know-how'. Over the summer of

---

[3]  Data on China's per capital GDP vary between sources (and bases for calculation). Rounded off, the $12,000 cited for 2022 is supported by the International Monetary Fund (IMF) and the Federal Reserve Bank.

1851, in London, the Great Exhibition of the Works of Industry of All Nations took place and was visited by more than six million people – equivalent to a third of the British population at the time. It was the first such major international exhibition of manufactured products and later inspired many others elsewhere. Its cash profit was then invested in the building of a set of museums, universities, and performance venues nearby, all of which have continued to pay tribute to the central role of knowledge in society. What the Great Exhibition symbolized was the culmination of an unusually fertile fusion of societal features building up over centuries and laying the groundwork for what would become an economic and social miracle. As Bradford DeLong (2022: 1) describes:

> The 140 years from 1870 to 2010 of the long twentieth century were . . . the most consequential years of all humanity's centuries. And it was the first century in which the most important historical thread was what anyone would call the economic one, for it was the century that saw the end of our near-universal dire material poverty.

It is furthermore highly significant that, for DeLong, 'it naturally stops in 2010' (2). So, this Element examines that compelling trajectory, and similar others that followed, so as to identify its shared determinants and to conjecture an explanation about the post-2010 loss of balance we now live with. Analysis now focusses on the socio-economic processes by which societies have historically achieved progress but which require constant transformation in a changing world.

The account will be set within the long-standing debates between visionaries such as Hayek (1979), for whom the competitive discipline of free markets drives progress but carries the later risk that allowing respect for those who break the code is no way to maintain a civilization, and of Polanyi (1944), who more generally argued that economic behaviour can only be properly understood as embedded in social influences. Heilbroner (1985) and McCloskey (2006, 2010, 2016) also stress the significance for progress of key virtues such as decency and benevolent authority; so too does Keynes (1933: 326) with his concern for the use of freedom to live 'wisely and agreeably and well'. As to the hiatus of 2010, it fits the pattern of Streeck's inevitable tension between economic and social forces and the difficulty of keeping them balanced. So, what more precisely is in the balance? And how might a society retain an achieved equilibrium while always moving with the times?

## The Crucial Role of Transformative Capacity

Given that volatility goes with built-in economic-social tensions, enough resilience to absorb it has always been a condition within any successful societal formula. To study capitalisms in terms of their evolutionary dynamics, then, allows specific cases to be understood as being at different phases in trajectories of resilience that are all bound by certain universal criteria for progress. Their adaptability so far is what has sustained their capacity for maintaining progress. Such an approach is seen by Streeck (2012: 22) as more revealing for the study of contemporary cases than is the study of the differences between them. Seeing them as living systems as such reveals how 'it is the dynamism that dictates the agenda of political choices, instead of the other way round'. Following Eisenstadt (1965), such adaptiveness rests on a societal capacity to critique its own sources of imbalance. This heightens the relevance of free thinking and the open exchange of informed knowledge, a theme also central to the parallel work of Mokyr (2002, 2009, 2017) on the role of societal knowledge in progress and of McCloskey (2006, 2010, 2016) on the role of the bourgeoisie in its ethical use. The former covers what to do; the latter covers how the doing of it is justified.

Under this conception of an 'always precarious' evolving complex system (Streeck 2012: 25) containing two balanced forces, there can be no assumption of a lasting normality coming to dominate, since the main forces driving its processes are in permanent tension; and in a changing world, such tension has perhaps been necessary, as the driver of adaptive progress in which mistakes, negative outcomes, fluctuating success, and new knowledge always threaten any achieved equilibrium. But when change happens, some societies learn better than others how to restore equilibrium, and the society continues to progress. By what processes does this constant and complex adjustment work?

The argument made here is that (at least so far in history), free-market democratic capitalism became the leading vehicle for carrying societal progress and that its greatest 'invention' was benevolent domination (Heilbroner 1985) applied to societal complexity at scale. In its application, this meant 'empowerment', such that, in day-to-day practice, owners/managers treat employees with respect, pay them reasonably, and provide them with opportunities to better themselves. The workforce gains a voice. In enacting these 'bourgeois virtues' (McCloskey 2006, 2010, 2016), managers additionally behave as good citizens more broadly. I refer again to Pinker's (2016) assumption that this response is also driven by certain universal psychological instincts about cooperation that human beings inherit at birth as members of a so far successfully evolved species.

To consider such ideas for their relevance today, Streeck proposes a form of 'economic sociology' to acknowledge Polanyi's (1944) embeddedness of economic action. After Geertz (1973), this approach is here termed 'thick description' (for its application, see Redding 2005) and it can be used in a complex adaptive systems framework that permits a focus on a society's evolved capacity to transform itself, such competence being anchored in day-to-day realities (here termed 'processes') that can be compared. Because this historical trajectory approach to explanation is rare, some further attention will be first paid to how this will be done.

## What Needs to Be Explained?

In terms of societal processes, civilizations tend to evolve by cohering around a system of beliefs shaped over time in a geography which itself may have shaped them. An example is the norm of centralized authority in societies dependent for their survival on the control of water sources (Welzel 2013). Because the responses required to support *continuous* progress are only rarely achieved in stable combination at societal scale, growth is often subject to interruptions. When progress does continue, it normally rests on a society's own endorsed stabilizing of coherent but resilient social order. Such order rests in turn on a fabric of reliable institutions; and these in turn need to be legitimated by a set of inspirational moral beliefs allowing authority to be perceived as essentially benevolent, ethical, and adaptive (Hacker 2021).

Given such conditions, it is common for a civilization to make progress with a high level of learning, including from others; forms of internal cooperativeness; a shared definition of virtue; and a capacity for transformation. The learning can also release new efficiencies in innovative resource use based on scientific knowledge. But, as the Nobel Prize–winning economist Michael Spence (2011: 41) observed, 'There is a bit of a mystery as to how these reinforcing growth dynamics get started and why they don't when they don't'. This account explores that mystery.

## Forces for Change

Societies can be seriously disturbed by change. When this involves a one-sided power advantage, some have suffered as a result, as did the Indigenous tribes of North America. Others took advantage of it, as did the many colonial powers. Change can be ideational, technical, or both. It can also be positive or negative. Examples of significant positive change include the following:

(1) In early mediaeval Europe, new techniques for forging metals at higher temperatures brought the iron plough to replace earlier wooden ones. This then allowed the use of deeper more fertile heavy soils and brought better agricultural yields. Spreading north from the Mediterranean, this new productivity contributed to the post-thirteenth-century surge in wealth,

exchange, and urbanization, with the latter providing the conditions for the Enlightenment and the Industrial Revolution of the nineteenth century (Baumard 2016).

(2) A rise in Christian ascetic and individualist ideals stabilized the ethics that accompanied that surge of wealth in mediaeval Europe.

(3) Benevolent political domination became theorized convincingly during the Enlightenment.

(4) The Newtonian understanding of the physical universe permitted the advances in astronomy and navigation that made possible much of European colonial expansion.

(5) Applied science such as Edison's breakthroughs in the application of electricity and their effects on light and on machinery brought new productivity to industry.

(6) Marx's reconceptualizing of societal authority relations contributed to the idea of the welfare state.

(7) The recent effects of information technology on communications and organization globally are changing the formulae for efficiency of many firms, economies, and societies.

## Response to Change

Since compatibility with established ideals and practices can vary, civilizations respond to innovation in different ways. This is especially relevant where established traditions affect the use of power, as when autocracy is perpetuated in a current economy. Condensed briefly as summary essentials, societal betterment has rested on three core capabilities:

(1) A culture which *inspires* citizens to see authority as essentially benevolent, morally responsible, and open to the influence of informed critical thinking.

(2) The capacity of a society to *transform* itself through ownership, innovation, adaptation, cooperativeness, and the balancing of interests.

(3) Forms of encouraged communicative action that foster *competitive productivity*, while also contributing to the evolution of a stable ethical order in the public interest, and are grounded in local norms.

## Cause and Effect

Since progress works in highly complex ways, it is also necessary to make clear certain assumptions made here about causation. *First*, societies are seen as complex adaptive systems. This permits the dynamism of their evolution to be seen through several specialized perspectives within a general theory. *Second*, the main determinants of societal evolution consist of multiple elements flowing together. These complex determinants are seen, following Ragin's (1987) advice on societal comparison, as 'fuzzy sets'. *Third*, within these sets the specific phenomena of interest in explaining how a society works are conceived not as institutions, values, and policies but as 'processes', eight of which are identified. These represent the essence of what goes on in daily action as people get things done using the institutions, motivated by the values, and building the order (see Figure 1). *Fourth*, the processes, seen as a full set, build the main societal capabilities responding to what are termed here the 'lessons of history', that is, what societies over centuries have found to work. These lessons are derived from several hundred studies of what has so far led to societal progress.[4] The processes are what have delivered the three key summary *capabilities* identified in the section 'Response to Change': an inspiring context, transformative capacity, and empowered action. Important conceptually is that the form of society that evolves is not seen as a finished product but a system always capable of adapting itself to a changing world. We are observing moving objects that need to retain their flexibility.

This account will then be as follows:

(1) The evolution of progressive types of society.
(2) The main types of capitalism so far evolved.
(3) Explaining patterns in societal progress.
(4) The lessons of history.
(5) A conceptual structure for societal process analysis.
(6) The cases of liberal market democratic capitalism, seen as 'Western'.
(7) The cases of state-based developmental capitalism exemplified by China.
(8) Lessons drawn from the comparisons.
(9) Implications for an uncertain future.

## 1 The Evolution of Progressive Types of Society

Over the ages of human habitation, the world has seen the evolution of three main types of society: (1) 'open' and 'inclusive', with high levels of cooperativeness and flexibility and a capacity for absorbing high complexity; (2) relatively 'closed', and often 'extractive', in which there is central control, limited spontaneous cooperative bonding, less flexibility, and less ability to effectively absorb the complexities that go with societal progress; and (3)

---

[4] A short selection is given in the References. Much larger studies are available, for instance in McCloskey (2016), Mokyr (2017), Pinker (2018), Galor (2022), and Koyama and Rubin (2022).

evolved hybrids combining aspects of both. The open and hybrid types tend to be more prosperous and to attract people to them. The second, more closed and autocratic, tend to be relatively less productive and less appealing to people accustomed to freedom but – especially when large – can still exert influence on others. It should be noted here that China has fluctuated radically over recent decades between the open and closed types and has displayed powerful efficiency and growth in certain phases. This Element now proposes a form of thick description based on a set of *processes within the workings of living societies*. Before defining them, we first consider the tendency for varied responses to evolve.

## Explaining Variety in Responses

For centuries, people have thought deeply about the idea of societal betterment and – as populations grew and states formed – about getting the most out of the assets available to them so as to better sustain their people. Early philosophies in the West came with classical Greek thinking and Roman law, all laying respected conceptual foundations that informed the Enlightenment. In pre-Chin China came the philosophies of Guanzi, Laozi, Confucius, Mencius, Mozi, Xunzi and Hanfeizi, seen widely as still relevant.

Added to these philosophies were the practical methods that emerged from the operating systems invented by administrators and by merchants as they traded more widely. In China, there came the record-keeping systems in the Western Zhou dynasty and the Tang system of Bi-Bu auditing.[5] In Europe came the systems of international banking (invented while sitting on a traders' bench, or *banco*) in twelfth-century Florence; the first passports invented at Tours in late mediaeval France to facilitate travel in Europe; the system of double-entry book-keeping by Pacioli in the same period; and the electing of a 'law merchant' to settle trading disputes at the annual Champagne fairs. Such systems of order evolved and were seen as helpful in reducing uncertainty, and they spread. Participants gained from the better predictability; authorities gained from the greater control and social stability. Regular gatherings allowed the sharing of new knowledge. Intermediate authorities, such as guilds licensed by states, emerged to guarantee the standards of compliance in their field of action. Legitimate order slowly accumulated, often from the ground up.

By the eighteenth century, as the complexity of issues grew with more global flows of commerce, Adam Smith's (1776) sophisticated analysis of the wealth of nations, showing the interactions between economic, social, and moral influences, provided a long-respected basis for later studies of societal progress.

---

[5] A form of enterprise auditing developed in the Tang dynasty (618–907 CE).

Other leading explanations from the more recent large literature on socio-economic history are – to select a few – Mokyr's (2017) 'culture of growth', McCarthy (2009) on 'the idea of human development', Acemoglu and Robinson's (2012) 'why nations fail', McCloskey's (2006) 'bourgeois virtues', and Pinker's (2018, 2021) celebrations of empowerment and of rationality. The question of evolved variety is addressed by Whitley (1999) in terms of firms in societies finding their own interpretations of how to organize, collaborate, and compete, as shaped by the surrounding formal norms about rights and duties and informal customs and ideals about acceptable practice. Looking forward, Bresser-Pereira (2017) sees the possibility of an amended form of capitalism that meets the currently rising needs for societal cohesion. This is reflected in new sensitivities favouring 'stakeholder capitalism' (Murray and Whitney 2022).

Following Acemoglu and Robinson (2012: 429), two key principles of explanation are suggested. First, 'a successful theory does not faithfully reproduce details, but provides an empirically-grounded explanation for a *range of processes* while also clarifying the main forces at work'.[6] Second, a crucial distinction needs to be made between *extractive* and *inclusive* economic and political institutions, the inclusive being 'more conducive to economic growth'. Given that extraction is normally by definition unethical, this issue also lies at the centre of Pinker's (2018, 2021) parallel theories about the role of empowerment through rationality and his summarizing of the Enlightenment contribution as 'knowledge and sound institutions lead to moral progress' (Pinker 2018: 228). As noted, Pinker (2016) has additionally emphasized the depth of influence of human instincts inherited at birth as an outcome of evolution. These continue invisibly to shape people's predispositions concerning trust, cooperativeness, and identity, and he warns that these cannot effectively be overridden by new formulae – often based on imposed conformity – that deny those deeper instincts.

The approach here suggests a *set of eight societal processes* (Figure 1), each containing many influences – economic, psychological, political, and sociological – flowing together within specific fields of action (Ragin's 'fuzzy sets'). An example would be how socio-economic cooperativeness works in – say – China as opposed to the United States. Each process explains one key aspect of the total workings of a socio-economy. *It is the positive nature of these processes, and the careful blending of them, that account for the relative success or failure in fostering overall societal progress.* Across the set, harmony, balance, and consistency with the deeper instincts of human nature are needed for the synergies involved to become fruitful.

---

[6] Emphasis my own.

In this multi-determinant complex adaptive system, two other main assumptions apply. First, every process has a part to play. A society which has weak development of one or more of the eight processes is likely to remain relatively handicapped. For instance, an over-controlling authority may inhibit the spontaneous evolving of new systems of order. A second assumption is that the essential roles of societal leadership are those of inspirational moral legitimating and then of balancing and coordinating. Such integrating releases synergies that can induce features distinct to a single society and help to support its viability as a total system competing with others. As an example of that, the form of close collaboration between government and industry in Japan is quite unique to that society and powerful in its effects. China's influential familism ideals hold many organizations together. So too more widely does investment capital flow into well-managed and trusted stock markets. And a geographical space such as Silicon Valley, designed to allow communicative action to flourish, becomes full of people collaborating. Such synergies can in turn release new creative energy that feeds into outcomes such as productivity per capita and technical breakthroughs. Each society will have its own total formula, its own way of inspiring and blending the eight processes, just as the conductor of a symphony orchestra, given highly trained members, blends the strings, brass, percussion, keyboard, and wind instruments within a score to produce a memorable shared experience that is usually distinct – and can be inspirational – for those hearing it as a totality.

Considering now the wider global context, the world has long been understood to contain a variety of social psychologies – the cognitive frameworks shaping behaviours that maintain a society's stability. It is enough here to state in preview that they particularly influence how authority is used and how cooperation works.

The realities of geography and history can also give rise to combinations that – if not entirely accidental – were often influenced by fortuitous timing. In the early 1800s, much stimulus to the first Industrial Revolution occurred when access by Britain to the resources of imperial India and elsewhere coincided with new thinking in science and politics. So too was China's post-1980 surge in growth influenced by the great reserves of available low-cost labour that coincided with a policy of opening the economy to world business. Societies can thus benefit from being both open to change and able to take opportunities when they are presented. Following Eisenstadt (1965), this crucial ability to adjust will be referred to as a society's 'transformative capacity'.

## 2 The Main Types of Capitalism So Far Evolved

Before introducing further detail on societal trajectories, it is first necessary to present the versions being taken here as models of success in progressing the quality of lives of their people. Since this achievement is about people making a living, it is commonly analysed in varying 'systems of capitalism' or 'business systems'. The processes within them reflect their societal legacies of context, culture, and history.

In a large empirical study of the world's business systems, and building on an extensive prior literature, Michael Witt et al. (2018) identified nine distinct forms which vary in their level of societal progress. Given the immense complexity faced, the categories were identified at a first-stage (i.e. institutional) level of comparative analysis. This covered sixty-one economies accounting for 94 percent of world GDP. The societal institutions studied were education, employment relations, finance, interfirm relations, firm dynamics, ownership and governance, social capital, and the role of the state. The forms of socio-economy that emerged from the analysis as distinct clusters are two socialist, twenty-one emerging, four oil-based, two advanced city, six advanced emerging, ten European peripheral, six liberal market, nine coordinated market, and one highly coordinated.

The analysis that follows pays tribute to the rigour of that study in categorizing the variety of societal business systems worldwide. It now adds a complementary perspective to that based mainly on institutions when explaining the workings of such systems. It examines the *processes within* the institutional structures/societal cultures and so compares societies as *living* complex adaptive systems. This then permits some 'thick description' of *how* they meet certain criteria for being progressive and shows the way the '*hows*' vary. The *hows* then have practical implications for future tendencies and for theory about variations in 'success'.

The labelling of the nine categories of socio-economy identified in the Witt and colleagues' research provides an initial guide to the basic character of each and is as follows (in no order of priority):

*Socialist*: Cuba and Venezuela as totalitarian states using a socialist ideology.
*Emerging*: twenty-one societies (including India, Russia, and China) at various stages of 'development' towards higher per capita wealth but not yet through the 'middle-income trap' that now cuts in at about PPP (purchasing power parity) US$20,000 per capita.[7]
*Arab oil-based*: four economies (excluded here from further analysis as being a special case).

---

[7] The middle-income trap is encountered when productivity per capita can only be increased through greater participation, creativity, and empowerment within the workforce, while these features are not fully developed or in decline (see Eichengreen et al. 2011).

*Advanced city*: Hong Kong and Singapore (today only Singapore due to radical
changes in Hong Kong since the analysis). The processes within this city-
based form might well also appear as relevant inside other geographies, as
with regional concentrations like Silicon Valley, the Bangalore complex, or
the Cambridge–Oxford–London triangle.

*Advanced emerging*: six economies, considered as progressive (Chile, Israel,
South Korea, South Africa, Taiwan, and Turkey).

*European peripheral*: ten, essentially southern/Latin/Catholic Europe.

*Liberal market*: six, the 'West' led by the United States, the United Kingdom,
Australia, and New Zealand.

*Coordinated market*: nine, essentially northern/Protestant mainland Europe.

*Highly coordinated*: Japan.

In what follows, for reasons of space, attention will mainly be given to comparing two archetypes: liberal market and state-directed developmental. Chosen for
their global significance, they have contrasting natures and histories with
a bearing on the current large shifts in the global context. The liberal market
capitalist versions are seen in summary as 'Western'. The state-directed versions within the *emerging* category are represented particularly in China and so
termed party-state-directed, a form with echoes in Russia, as well as in other
states controlled within a dominant ideology. Brief note will be taken of the
evolving of hybrids, an example of which is the historically hybridized Japan
and the state-led but democratic *advanced city* form visible in Singapore. The
remaining variety contained within the two main types is acknowledged but can
only be briefly examined; they may, however, be seen as hybrid forms of the
main alternative types: the liberal market and the state-directed. As process-
based societal comparison is rare, certain principles of method and explanation
will first be clarified.

## 3 Explaining Patterns in Societal Progress

Because of the complexity of the objects of study, certain conceptual issues
arise. What kind of 'causation' is appropriate to explain the differences
between the societal systems? How might a society's progress be predeter-
mined historically? How do we compare across different socially constructed realities, including the often invisible workings of influences such
as power and knowledge? The compatibility of ends and means also brings
in the question of balancing across the many processes involved. These
issues will now be considered so as to help us understand how they are
implied and embraced within the complex adaptive systems theory being
proposed.

## Causation

There are two broad sources of influence on societal progress: those which are external and internal to the workings of a socio-economy. The external influences are the 'givens' of geography and of world history, over which a society has no choice, as with the climate, what crops can be grown, and what resources found. Size and location are also important 'givens', for instance Singapore's location as a hub on crucial trading routes or the range of geographical environments and resources within (and under) the great land area of the United States. The first Industrial Revolution in the nineteenth century was popularly explained by Britain's new industries being founded on coal and surrounded by fish. Russia's current influence rests on its natural resources. Such determinants are non-negotiable givens.

The second set is of more 'negotiable' influences – this time internal and administrative. They derive from how the society itself comes to organize the work and lives of its citizens. Such negotiable influences become the main focus for the rest of this account. Study of them will illustrate one significant overriding contrast affecting a society's ability to transform and advance: the sharing of power. For instance, is authority to decide matters widely dispersed throughout an informed and listened-to public? Or is it monopolized within an elite with decisions imposed and enforced by control? There is no doubt that in some circumstances the centralizing of power works well, but in the modern context of globalized industry, hyper complexity, increasingly specialized knowledge and skill, fast innovation, instant communication, and high-speed transactions, does monopolized control reduce the quality and adequacy of competitive response to the new complexity?

We will later also note that economic historians find patterns in societal progress whereby the waves of advancement slow down and level off, unless rising complexity can be accommodated by societal transformation based on new thinking about appropriate responses. Dependence on the borrowing of know-how may prove to be a temporary solution, since practical know-how may be easier to acquire than the knowledge behind it. But, regardless of how, transformative capacity always remains crucial and it always eventually comes from learning, commonly enriched by the wider spread of knowledge across a society. The most fundamental issues relating to this are, firstly, how power comes to be used to facilitate the growth of knowledge and, secondly, the societal responsiveness to change – issues that keep rising in significance. In summary, on causation there is a wide and complex set of causes and a continuous need to acknowledge their combined effects.

## Path-Dependence

In comparing societies, it is also necessary to take account of another significant – but invisible – force that links the present with the society's inheritance, since it adapted to foster its people's survival in distinct geographical/ecological conditions. When strong authority was needed to ensure group survival, then centralized power became normal and legitimate. Embedded in the society's culture this effect can be carried forward over millennia. It is not accidental that for all its history China has always had an emperor figure and why most African and Latin American societies also rely on strong central leadership.

The deepest study of this effect has been by Welzel (2013). Briefly summarized, each society evolved over millennia in a 'culture zone', with its own climate and landscape. As Welzel demonstrates, a society's 'culture zone' of climate and the geography 'sits at the beginning of a chain of developments from surplus agriculture, to urban civilization, to technological advancement . . .. Civilization requires the existence of surplus agriculture to feed urban populations. This is where climatic conditions matter' (123). Key questions are then: what makes surplus agriculture possible in the first place? How is the surplus produced? And how large is that surplus at a given level of technology?

Other factors then affect the options. In the humid tropical river valleys where people in early civilizations tended to concentrate, as in the valleys of the Nile, the Euphrates, or China's river valleys, the soil fertility depended on the additions of new silt brought with regular flooding. As populations grew, urban citizens required access to staple food crops such as rice, which carries with it heavy investment in labour and controlled access to water. In such constricted areas, those needs could only be met with disciplined forms of social control to manage the necessary irrigation and flood control. For these reasons, the original 'warm water' tropical river-valley civilizations that emerged over millennia were all based on *regimented allotment* cultivation and *water control*, under *coercive feudalism*. To remain viable, such societies evolved under strong central hierarchy and their cultures legitimized that response ideologically. A fundamental authoritarianism became central to the culture and remains deeply ingrained.

Different societal forms evolved later, as in north-western Europe, in environments with a combination of cooler overall temperatures and regular light rainfall. These sparsely populated and partly forested spaces permitted the addition of hunting and gathering to the settled family-based farming and produced a 'categorically different type of surplus agriculture' (Welzel 2013: 124). The social structure – adapted in part to deal with societal defence – became *contractual feudalism*, requiring agreement between the parties. This in turn brought with it a culture where the organization of labour fitted within a lord–peasant relation that was far less hierarchical than in the tropical contexts.

In the temperate 'cool water' environments with regular light rainfall, survival did not depend on organized irrigation. With widely scattered small populations, there was no shortage of farming land, so family units were in many respects self-sustaining and independent. The surplus land brought additional food sources from hunting and gathering, options which encouraged ideals of voluntary sharing, reciprocity, and social community beyond family. With ingrained habits of autonomy and freedom, individuals would later contend for rights, and this latter cultural tradition became absorbed as the defining 'individualism' and 'freedom' of the several Western cultures of civilization that would over millennia evolve in such regions before later spreading further, most notably to North America. Colonial extensions would carry the same ideals elsewhere and contribute to the modifying of some political systems voluntarily where power-sharing had not been culturally inherited. The two different ancient legacies are still there in their effects. The warm water societies inherit autocracy in their cultures. The cool water societies inherit norms of authority based on consent. And there can be hybrids of the two.

The distinct ancient survival response in most tropical ecologies remains still visible in the social cultures and personal mindsets described by George Foster (1967) as the surrounding reality of most agriculture-based existence in the tropics today. At its cultural core is 'an image of limited good' echoed more recently for China by Shambaugh (2013), who observes that the total amount of 'good' available in the society is seen as fixed and will not grow. Life then becomes a 'zero-sum game': if one person gains something, then it comes from others losing the same amount. Sensitivities to reciprocity then become heightened. This brings a distinct pattern to the behaviours to be later considered under the theme of 'cooperativeness'. The implicit fatalism then makes authority more tolerable.

The two main political alternatives of democracy and authoritarianism then have quite different ancient origins, and those prehistoric influences remain embedded as norms in today's cultures. This suggests why, as noted, China appears always to 'need' an emperor figure, as also do many African and Middle Eastern cultures. Western Europe over time evolved differently towards shared power, where central authority tends to be held only symbolically. As a cultural extension of that, the United States was formed to be cohesive without royalty. Japan and the United Kingdom, by different routes, found it advantageous to retain the structural and symbolic unifying influence of an inherited head of state but one whose direct power had been limited. Studies of cultural difference show that social hierarchy is among the most fundamental elements within the contrasting systems of meaning around which realities remain societally constructed (Inglehart and Welzel 2005; Inglehart 2018). Its effects are visible in the 'empowerment' contrasts seen by Pinker (2018) as crucial in determining societal progress. Alternative forms of authority are also evident in the structures of economic coordination that have evolved to form the world's different business systems (Whitley 1999; Redding 2005; Witt and Redding 2014).

There has also been a historic rise in the complexity that societies must deal with as processes of economic exchange proliferate exponentially. So too, even more easily, does information now threatening by being artificial. So, perceptions and expectations about choice expand – and change accelerates. Several key questions then arise for societies that continue to express anciently founded ideals of central control and imposed discipline. Can they evolve from their inherited socialization and adjust into a form that depends less on control and more on devolved initiative and civic responsibility? If so, can they find a stable and effective way of releasing the individual creative energies connected with higher levels of competitive productivity – the ultimate economic test of societal capacity to progress? Will any newly invented way of coordinating a socio-economy be compatible with the fundamental 'lessons of history' so far (to be summarized shortly) about how societal progress has actually been achieved? Will those lessons of history need to be rewritten? These questions will run here as a subtext and will add to the scrutiny of the main theme: the crucial contribution of a society's 'transformative capacity' to its progress. In simple terms: can it learn?

The limits to societal progress that path-dependent central control can bring are visible in the daily news, as some societies show signs of 'capture' by dominant individuals: see any account of China's cultural revolution (e.g. Dikotter 2010) or Russia's invasion of Ukraine. Consider how Communist ideals about equality so predictably lead to totalitarianism because 'the vast economic researches of Marx did not even touch the problems of a constructive economic policy, for example economic planning ... did not even study what the so-called "bourgeois economists" attained in this field' (Popper 1962: 83). As Pinker (2016) contends, people are born with inherited instincts of the species that need to be responded to rather than replaced with something engineered elsewhere within narrow logics.

To balance things out, consider how societies that are otherwise 'open' also need to learn lessons. But even if open societies are more likely to learn, they can still be vulnerable to the misunderstanding of others' covert realities. This issue is as much disputed as it is opaque. As analysed by Friedberg (2022) in regard to US-China misunderstandings, China is judged an irresponsible stakeholder in global interests. This is in turn disputed by Bergsten (2022), who sees China as more revisionist than revolutionary and a moderate potential partner in the pursuit of global interests. The two socially constructed realities do not overlap, nor do the analyses of them.

A conclusion by Ferguson (2011: 95) on the progress of civilizations provides a convenient setting for the specific case explanations that will follow. His view is that the West became distinguished from 'the Rest' by inventing six 'identifiably novel complexes of institutions and associated ideas and behaviours' (12), namely competition, science, property rights/law/votes, medicines, the consumer society, and the work ethic. Within that set of contrasts, he then expands on what he means by 'property rights' and asks: 'Can a non-Western power really hope to benefit from downloading Western scientific knowledge, if it continues to reject that other part of the West's winning formula: the third institutional innovation of private property rights, the rule of law, and truly representative government?'

So, I close this consideration of long-term path-dependencies by carrying forward Ferguson's six civilizational principles, to build them into a fuller explanation of societal progress. Thus progress will eventually rest on two related fundamental issues: how can authority be best attuned to the inherited human instincts? And by what defining of virtue can a society's morality provide as much social as individual benefit? In other terms, how can the natural response of self-interest that grows in zero-sum societies be supplanted by an inspiring ideal of public good adopted as a means of progress? Before considering such questions, it is first necessary to note there being, as just inferred, no single global 'reality'. Societies are lived in as different worlds (Berger and Luckmann 1966). This is an important qualifier when comparing their workings, their interactions, and their possible views of other societies.

## Different Socially Constructed Realities

For a society to escape from a mindset of limited good and adopt an optimistic ideal of 'progress' can prove to be a very long-term challenge since the amount of good needs first to be understood as expandable. To grow an 'inspirational context' is often also a matter of the catalysts that identify and inspire it: America's New Deal, China's dream of common prosperity, Singapore's meritocracy, and Britain's distinct symbol of royal public virtue.

In more grounded terms, the most common catalyst for societal inspiration has been knowledge-based technical innovation. Such a breakthrough is described by Slack (2015) in his study of 'the invention of improvement' in seventeenth-century England, over which period the national GDP per capita doubled. Expansion then continued into the first Industrial Revolution based on productivity-driven prosperity. New industrial cities absorbed the population as it grew from 6.1 million in 1600 to 31.4 million in 1870. During that long early surge, per capita wealth also grew from $973 to $3,184 in 1990 international dollars (Maddison 2007). Societal 'good' was visibly expanding. So too was 'participation'. So too was the understanding of what was happening. Reality was being redefined, and that included a shared view of what could be possible. For 'good' to escape from being perceived as limited, a new more optimistic reality had first to become both normal and inspirational.

Accounts of such progress in Europe (Slack 2015; Baumard 2016), as noted, show that it began with the discovery of methods to increase yield in agriculture, such as deep ploughing, crop rotation, fertilizers, and new patterns of devolved land ownership. The word 'improvement' is Anglo-Norman in origin and a thousand years ago came into use to describe the initial turning of land into profit by cultivation. That made some surplus available and with that would emerge a shared optimism about growth and an understanding that new knowledge could contribute new efficiency and new wealth. Significantly, Baumard sees this set of forces as the origin of fairness, in that such an integrating public ideal could not evolve until the problem of perceived limited good had faded away. Reality was redefined by there being enough for everyone plus more. This prosperity-based optimism would grow as a psychological foundation for the first Industrial Revolution. Its effects would then bring what Mokyr (2017) sees as a new 'culture of growth'.

This new reality would later be further transformed during its industrial Victorian expansion when it led to the first railway, the biggest ship ever then built, and the first 'workshop of the world'. Science-backed technology had become the leading catalyst for progress; and it has continued to determine the influences that have driven the consequent separating out of societies in terms of prosperity.

It is then appropriate to acknowledge the consequences that flow from this optimistic and inspiring force in the wider arena of competing civilizations. Its most significant catalyst is productivity, as the use of know-how adds to what an average day's work can yield. Welzel et al. (2017) cite research by Gallop et al. (1999) showing that productivity per capita in the 'cool water' areas is four times higher than in the tropics and three times higher than in dry areas. Combined with the psychology of empowerment that stems from relative family autonomy over resources, as well as a custom of debate and open critical thinking, such ecological conditions correlate (at 0.73 over 142 societies) with the greater technological and financial capacities that evolved in some societies over time.

## Ends and Means

A final point on method for studying anything so complex comes from a review of 'progress studies' by Bartley Madden (2020), who concludes that sustainable capitalism and societal progress can only be achieved through the coordinating of ends and means. In straightforward terms, ends are ideals to be attained in the future, whereas means are practical and in the present. When asking whether an end justifies the means, questions may arise about morality or cost-efficiency. I simply note here that ends and means are distinct from each other and that inadequate attention to their being compatible can lead to confusion both practical and theoretical. For example, if a society aims to have high levels of innovativeness in its industry, then the means of achieving that condition are likely to include individual creative freedoms, habits of non-conformity, and the wide availability of knowledge as well as incentive. Some oddballs in the laboratory may need to be tolerated as appropriate means to make the scientific breakthroughs that are a society's ends. Compatibility then implies balance and this lies at the centre of the theory being proposed.

In the present account, the most fundamental 'end' of interest is not so much the society's eventual GDP score but the prior condition that 'delivers' such progress, namely the society's *capability to learn* and so to adjust what it does and how it does it, and then make it able to respond effectively to changing circumstances. This is what makes reachable the other intentions within progress.

In all this complexity, the overall ends being served express a society's vision, this being the catalyst for its motivating power, realism, and widespread personal endorsement. It is why great leaders are remembered for what they first defined and then achieved. Joel Mokyr's (2009: 1) classic study of the first Industrial Revolution is relevant here, with his view on how a change in 'ends' drove it forward to permit its enormous nineteenth-century power. As he saw the adjusting of the ends–means link, a 'positive feedback loop created the greatest sea-change in economic history since the advent of agriculture' (1). Identifying a combination of prior Enlightenment thinking and Christian ideals, and paying tribute to David Hume's (1758) singling out of knowledge and ethics as keys to progress, Mokyr (2009) explains that in Britain more than anywhere else at that time there was a coordinated countermovement against the ancient privileges and monopolies earlier acquired by the elite and known somewhat obliquely as 'freedoms'. These had accreted especially in the expanding foreign and colonial trade and in incorporated towns, apprenticed labour, and rent-seeking generally. But there also emerged a capacity to transform, and new thinking among those with influence would bring curbs to the earlier advantages. By the 1830s, a new order had evolved with renewed ethics, and the traditional bases of power were slowly dismantled (Heffer 2013).

Over time, this new order would exhibit the workings of one of the core processes in the schema shown in Figure 1, namely the leadership's seeking of balance across the society's processes. Mokyr (2009: 426–7) sees an example of this balancing in the 1792 delegation to China led by Lord Macartney in the hope of opening up the China market for British products. This showed that an exclusive elite could also display the commercial initiative to lead the many processes that would later bring sustained economic development by the society's entrepreneurs. As he then observes, 'It is this kind of dynamic that created the success that allowed the growth of useful knowledge and technological ingenuity to become the foundation of sustained economic development' (427).

So, the first Industrial Revolution evolved in a period of open debate and critical thinking that saw its purposes redefined. The adopted 'ends' would change from supporting the extraction of wealth by landlords into the wider acquisition and distribution of wealth. Relevant new means would then evolve, as with the widespread provision of education and welfare. Moral responsibilities became highly relevant. The classic explanation by Adam Smith of *The Wealth of Nations*, published in 1776, was preceded in 1759 by his *Theory of Moral Sentiments*. As a moral philosopher, his view was that market-based efficiency came about most naturally when the 'invisible hand' could do its work in conditions where the logics of free competition were in rational use by ethically responsible people devoted to enhancing the public good. This allowed an escape from the prior world of 'limited good'. Seen more completely, new ends would bring new means, with the entire transformation evolving to the extent made possible by the flow of knowledge-based understanding and free thinking, with societal processes evolving more widely in distinct historical circumstances, responding to distinct cultural heritages and surrounded by incoming influences from other societies and from technology.

To summarize now on principles of explanation, the conceptual issues which shape the approach taken here for comparing societal progressions are: causation is complex, with many interconnecting processes determining what happens in any one society; many societies show traces of ancient 'programming' of mindsets embedded in their culture from their early origins; people live in mental worlds socially constructed during their upbringing and these differ between societies; and it is necessary to achieve cohesion between ends and means when implementing action.

Under those four assumptions relating to method of analysis, I now turn to summarize the received wisdom about societal progress expressed in the research-based literature carried in several disciplines: economics, socioeconomics, political science, international business, development theory, and comparative capitalism.

## 4 The Lessons of History

The following ideas, common in the literatures on societal progress, may originally have been expressed in other terms but the concepts imagined by their authors fit nevertheless within the meanings suggested here. Inevitably, most theorists focus on a particular theme, and so the following list is an amalgam of contributions, all of which are relevant to the wide issue that unites them: how do some societies evolve more effectively than others to raise the quality of their people's lives?

These conjectured lessons will then be carried forward as criteria against which to judge the processes whereby a society responds to these universal patterns in human history so far. Such an approach coincides with the advice noted at the outset from Streeck (2012) that the crucial understanding needs to be of a society's *dynamism* (i.e. its processes) as it evolves, rather than its *difference* from competing alternatives. Only then can its socio-economy be acknowledged as 'embedded' in its own history. With that understanding, we now turn to a summary of the universal 'lessons of history' that underpin how those various dynamisms have been achieved:

(1) Societies – if they progress – evolve as complex adaptive systems by *constantly learning and changing*, or otherwise becoming relatively static.

(2) If they prosper, complexity within them becomes more dense and needs to be absorbed within *new forms of order*. The brainstorming and implementing of such new order can be effectively 'crowdsourced' (DeLong 2022: 448) from key actors in the socio-economy behaving in the public interest and rewarded by social respect. Scale is a challenge in this context, and forms of concentration – as in a city or a trade – can help to foster both debate and cohesion about the order needed. In many developed societies, much societal stability in trades, professions, and regulations has ancient origins from this devolved process of building order.

(3) Norms encouraging the *empowerment* of people will positively influence adaptiveness and in turn the competitive viability of societal systems. Creativity and initiative are released most fruitfully under conditions of ethical authority perceived as benevolent. If this obstacle is not overcome, growth normally slows and stops at around US$20,000 per capita GDP.

(4) The accidents of *relations between states* may strongly influence a society's accumulating heritage of responses.

(5) The overall patterns of determinacy seen in the abstract as universally valid may be interpreted and *applied in distinct ways* society by society.

(6)  Societal cohesion and cooperativeness rest heavily on *moral norms* that influence identity, dependency, and obligations towards the common good or 'civicness'. This process is enhanced by the predictability that comes with legitimate law over property and stable institutions.

(7)  For a society to become 'developed' starts with a *belief that it is possible*. Many limitations are buried deep within socially constructed realities, especially when these are framed within perceptions of limited good. As handicaps, these are reported for many developing societies.

(8)  Freely reasoned and informed *critical thinking* and openly rational debate can stimulate motivation, inventiveness, and productivity as well as build a society's stock of both pure and applied knowledge. The more that people can think for themselves, and communicate, the better is a society equipped to deal with change.

(9)  Networks matter. '*Communicative action*' between informed and engaged people encourages intellectual, technical, and commercial dynamism, as well as adaptiveness, in ways that support the growth of societal order, shared morality, related ideals of civicness, and the use of applied knowledge. This works best when legitimized by societal authority.

(10)  The political role is essentially one of *balancing the economic and societal* forces and interests while providing a *unifying vision* through which individual motivation, societal cooperation, and identity can become inspired. This works most effectively when the societal leadership is respected for its manifest wisdom and selfless virtue.

## 5 A Conceptual Structure for Societal Process Analysis

Reviewing the approaches of key theorists of societal progress, Goldthorpe (2021) takes special note of Popper's (1994: 144) cautioning about frameworks of explanation in which too much is left to 'the rationality principle' and not enough to the more crucial analysis of 'the situation itself'. As noted at the outset, such 'thick description' allows a society to be understood in depth. Drawing also on the work of Coleman (1990) on the foundations of social theory, in which attention is directed to the constant flow of influences between the macro and micro levels of a society, Goldthorpe concludes by recommending research to focus on the middle-range space of enquiry that links the levels of institutions and of action. In this, 'the aim is to identify specific mechanisms, in the form of social processes driven by individual action, that are capable of producing the phenomenon under investigation' (Goldthorpe 2021: 204). The account that follows is guided by that advice. Echoing it also Acemoglu and Robinson (2012), in studying societal success and failure, pay specific attention to a *set of societal processes*, the workings of which can be described for the different societies.

## Identifying the Crucial Processes

When progress is considered as achieved, it is normally judged as having made better the quality of life for a society's people. This outcome is most straight-forwardly represented in the UN's Human Development Index, which reports detailed global findings on health, education, and standard of living, including income, and takes account of features such as gender discrimination. In its 2020 report, 18 of the top 20 countries out of 189 were northern European in origin either directly or by direct heritage, such as the United States and Australia. The global variety is also visible in the differences between capitalisms referred to described on page 17. Seen objectively in terms of aspects of delivered societal quality, the UN's Human Development Index also reflects the sharing of wealth, the providing of welfare, security, and opportunity, and the releasing of the society's store of potential creativity and talent by the enhancement and sharing of its knowledge-based understanding. The large literature on 'empowerment' provides much of the rationale behind such criteria.

As suggested, a society's collective 'brain' tends to determine the shared quality of life through the processes of education, literacy, and debate. Not encouraging a society's brain power may result in a more convenient context for domination but does not help it to deal with the many complex societal accomplishments associated with the cooperative releasing and channelling of human energy. For that we need to include its moral base – Sissay's societal 'heart' – or in some accounts its 'soul' (Hacker 2021).

So what is a society's soul? It lies invisible but eventually traceable in the way the instinctive tendencies of *Homo sapiens* as a species are inspired and acted out in daily exchanges and eventually in more complex social structures. As Ridley (1996: 249), in his study of the origins of virtue, says, 'our minds have been built by selfish genes, but they have been built to be social, trustworthy, and cooperative'. Pinker (2016) cites a list of 300 deep human instincts that all members of the *Homo sapiens* species are born with. No other species has gone so far down this evolutionary path and built such integrated and effective forms of society, the ultimate beneficiaries being 'our masters – the genes'. These latter have secured – over millennia – the expansion of our brains and so our inventiveness. Our societies and minds have evolved together, each reinforcing trends in the other. Especially does the depth and range of our instinctive cooperativeness – 'the very hallmark of humanity' – set us apart from other animals.

As suggested earlier in summarizing the lessons of history, the authoritarian suppression of many genetic instincts risks the fracturing of that cooperativeness. Holding it together on the other hand can be most naturally inspired by selfless virtue in leadership, whose role is to symbolize duty to the public good. It is this espoused morality that can spread into the society as its 'heart' or 'soul'. As McCloskey (2006) has explained in detail for the business world, the 'bourgeois virtues' act as the cement holding together and sustaining the cooperativeness and the ethics within it.

In Hacker's (2021: 310) analysis of the workings of morality, a society's soul is what makes it a good place to live. When that is achieved, humans have created conditions in which there exist:

(1) the transcending of selfishness and the dedication to justice and the welfare of others
(2) self-realization in worthy roles
(3) creative labour
(4) a cultivated sense of aesthetics and appreciation of nature
(5) developed powers of reasoning in seeking understanding
(6) acceptance of suffering.

And, as later evolutionary inputs in some notably successful cases:

(7) equality as a condition of obedience
(8) freedom to think as a requirement for reasoning.

Hacker further observes the danger of regressions, as when in the third to fifth centuries Christian fanaticism destroyed the culture of Rome, in the sixteenth and seventeenth centuries Europe tore itself to pieces in wars of religion, and in the twentieth century mankind surpassed itself in evildoing.

In the face of rising complexity, societies – guided subliminally by the above instincts and subject to the societal capacity for transformation – can learn to invent and adopt improvements that make their progress more likely. Such reforms exist in many modes: votes for all, universal education, press freedom, non-discrimination, and more. People's learning from their own experience can also be enhanced by ideas absorbed from others, just as Japan centuries ago absorbed both Buddhist and Confucian ideals from China and then later, in the Meiji period, modern institutions from the West, or, equally, when Western Europe long ago adopted many ideals from the earlier civilizations of Greece and Rome and later a system of numbering from the Arab world. In more recent times, the joint-stock limited liability company, invented in its present form in the United Kingdom in 1856, came to have great influence on economic systems globally. The spreading continues both ways, and Japanese youth rituals of cosplay have recently gone global, as has Chinese Cantopop and Korean hallyu (Redding 2021), each of them opening up new perspectives for the young. Among all such conceptual transformations, perhaps the most far-reaching for human development globally since the era of classical Greece has been the rethinking about society that occurred and spread during the European 'Enlightenment' of the eighteenth century.

Widespread learning – if it occurs – can lead a society to build up a *transformative capacity* (Eisenstadt 1965) and so comply with perhaps the most significant finding from studies of societal complexity and progress. As expressed by Nicolis and Prigogine (1989: 242), 'the adaptive possibility of societies is the main source allowing them to survive in the long term, to innovate of themselves, and to produce originality'. As in nature, evolution proceeds by adaptation not only within the individual but as shared instincts in a social collectivity at any scale. In the case of a complex human society, the challenge is to create a means of transformation constructed by people holding informed opinions and with individual will moderated by civic consciousness. This response entails the inspiring and co-opting of many minds and influences. Historically, it tended to rest on a bed of religious ideals. More recently, some of these have become vulnerable to new thinking brought by the explosions of access to knowledge. This can often disturb the long-accumulated legitimacy of core ideals.

Having transformative capacity on its own is therefore not enough to ensure a society's stable progress. It can only work effectively to that end when accompanied by the other two main clusters of processes: *inspiration* and *empowered action*. Then progress that includes change can be stable enough to be reassuring, to accumulate, and even perhaps to be aspirational as in a national 'dream'. Having hitch-hiked around the United States as an English university student for several months in 1957, I can attest to the persuasive, kind, and cohesive optimism of 'the American dream' as it was being lived out at that time, and since expressed in lifelong friendships, as well as in regular political reaffirmations there.

But societies vary. Having for some decades taught executives in China, I can attest that the central ideal most of them hold is the ethic of personal *guanxi* relationships. Having also for some years taught their Russian equivalents in St Petersburg, I can attest to their regularly expressed concern over endemic societal mistrust. Dreams are not always reassuring. But other students over years in Zurich and Stockholm and Canberra tended to express a calm confidence about their context, so too in France and the United States.

To see societal quality in negative terms, examples abound of societies that restrict people's thinking and influence. In such cases, boundaries based on dogma are applied that stop people from sharing curiosity with others. Commonly an elite, using an ideology purporting to favour all, then retains domination through disempowerment, in the most unethical cases taking disproportionate advantage for themselves. Known as 'extraction', this latter effect is pointedly summarized by Acemoglu and Robinson (2012: 398) in their global study of the origins of prosperity: 'Nations fail economically because of extractive institutions.' They describe how elites – regardless of their noble ideologies – can 'design institutions in order to enrich themselves and perpetuate their power at the expense of the vast majority of people in society'. The corruption in China faced by Xi Jinping in 2012 is described in detail by Ang (2020: 210) as a paradox for its coinciding with an economic boom, but Ang concludes that the subsequent cutting off of society from the monitoring of corruption crippled the formation of civic qualities and China followed a path of attempted transformation very different from those successful elsewhere.

## Defining the Processes

Distilling out now the key themes within the various literatures, the suggested core processes that build a society's progress are seen in the three clusters shown in Figure 1. These processes would be enacted in ways distinct in each society, namely:

*An inspiring context* by (a) setting an example of selfless virtue sufficiently benevolent to encourage people to be decisive, to risk, and to own and (b) the encouragement of freely reasoned critical thinking and discourse so as to raise the quality of shared understanding of issues that arise as complexity increases.

*Transformative capacity* by (c) encouraging innovation, adaptiveness, and creativity; (d) providing ideals and forms of identity around which people can build cooperativeness with a moral base; and (e) balancing the interests that evolve to prevent discrimination and extraction.[8]

*Empowered action* by the practicalities of (f) encouraging flows of exchange and discussion between the key providers of new knowledge and the entrepreneurs and investors able to apply the knowledge to the benefit of the society; (g) fostering the spontaneous evolution of administrative order that protects the society against extraction and reduces uncertainty; and (h)

---

[8] Balance is needed in two contexts. At the total system level, the societal leadership is charged with the orchestration of the entire set of contributing processes. This entails the balancing of all societal interests. At a lower level of context, transformation works best when the contributions to it at ground level are also in balance and therefore stable in their mutually supportive workings.

growth via competitive productivity as the underlying test of both social meritocracy and the efficient allocation of resources.

Because of the blending implicit in their interflowing nature as they support societal functions, the clusters of *inspiring, transforming*, and *empowering action* are seen here as vectors of their component elements. To illustrate how such component processes flow together in a vector, *transformative capacity* builds up when a society contains processes of *innovativeness, cooperativeness, and balance*. Examples of these in practice are networks that exchange information about new technologies or opportunities; good relations with sources of finance; support for research and development; available technical knowledge; ideals of reciprocity that serve to make information and plans trustworthy; reputational ethics that prevent the abuse of others and protect societal good; and an inclination to take risk. When working together harmoniously, processes such as these determine whether a society achieves a capacity for transformation. If the transformation issue in question is larger, as for instance when it has political implications, then other processes such as critical thinking need to be co-opted to permit action of the kind that has produced several societal breakthroughs to the modern condition of societally stable high complexity. In an example noted earlier in discussing transformation, the British Industrial Revolution benefitted from a long slow reduction in the influence of the traditional elite.

Influencing the long-term viability of the entire societal system is the overriding leadership function that provides the inspiration to support the intended constant progressive forward movement. As that tends to imply transformation, its vector also connects with the crucial societal leadership process of *balanced orchestration* so as to maintain cohesion and cross-fertilization between the various interests as the society evolves.

## The Challenge of Instability

History shows two common, and usually connected, risks causing imbalance. The first is *extraction*, or the abuse of the system by special interests, suggesting inadequate built-in controls. The second (and often related) is *domination* through disempowerment and the prevention of free thinking and spontaneous contribution, usually with the justification of needing to preserve order. Societies handicapped in these ways can for a time retain their habits and might keep going – not so much on their quality as societies in the terms suggested in the previous section but on the using up of the resources available to them as long as they last: financial, natural, and human.

The arrival of a society at a point of slowdown in progress is a well-known historical phenomenon and has inspired different theories: Cardwell's law describes the negative influence of political domination on spontaneous change when responding to the new complexity (Cardwell 1972); the middle-income trap (Eichengreen et al. 2011) describes the effects of a gradual loss of societal energy capable of dealing with the higher levels of technical and administrative complexity met at around US$20,000 per capita gross national product (GNP); Kleiber's law (West 2017) explains the growth of cities as dependent on social interactions building returns to scale, so as to supplement the economies of scale that come from system size itself. Such networking benefits are clearly visible in Silicon Valley, the north Switzerland–south Germany axis, or the Oxford–Cambridge–London triangle; the Lewis (1954) turning point occurs when supplies of low-cost labour run out and this reduces industrial competitiveness. Explanations such as these address different aspects of societal change that demand transformation between the established stabilities of the pre-modern condition and the new flexibilities demanded by the modern. This change brings with it greater complexity, faster innovation, and the higher risks that accompany its greater opportunities. The society becomes challenged to make maximum use of the brainpower it contains.

A significant and growing influence affecting societal progress is the mastery of technology, a highly complex issue involving the often problematic dependence on technology in alliance building,[9] with the parallel risk of abuse via technology theft. As argued more fully by Hopf and Allen (2018: 6), 'the dynamics of hegemonic stability and transition are poorly understood'. Assuming that the deciding factor is the perceived use or abuse of power by and within the hegemon, the masses would seem well able to use their own judgement, as when they choose migration to where power is not abused. The top ten countries receiving migrants are Switzerland, Canada, Germany, the United Kingdom, Japan, Sweden, Australia, the United States, France, and the Netherlands (Reach Immigration 2019).

We may now apply the framework in Figure 1 to consider the workings of the vectors of processes in different societal systems. The comparison will be of two archetypes: the liberal market democratic 'Western' form and the party-state-industry developmental form represented in its China version. Brief note will also be taken of other cases and of certain successful hybrids.

Three overarching requirements for progress will frame the comparisons: (1) whether or not a society's political authority represents a morally legitimated and benevolent ideology that inspires the balanced orchestration of the forces and processes at work; (2) the society's evolved competence to transform itself

---

[9]  In the early days of shock when the United States discovered that the Russians could build better space rockets, Bob Hope reassured his audiences that the simple truth was 'their Germans are better than our Germans'.

to meet the forces of change; and (3) the releasing of initiatives in action that will lead to fruitful creative exchange, spontaneously evolved benevolent order, and competitive productivity.

## 6 Liberal Market Democratic Capitalism

Performance on overall societal progress, as seen by the United Nations Development Programme (UNDP), occurs in clusters of societies, one of which – the liberal market form – currently leads the world in successfully breaking through the invisible barrier to the 'modern'. This cluster provides a human experience that somehow in turn maximizes the productivity that increases the value available from using a society's assets. The extra value then pays for the welfare. The combination of individual freedom, freely debated ethics, and shared benefits also becomes magnetic, as visible in the informal but very telling measure of such societies being the most preferred destinations for migrants, who do not uproot themselves without reason.

This clustering of success is attributed by Eisenstadt (1965) to societal transformative capacity: the ultimate test of its ability to progress. The capacities for learning, cooperating, and adjusting are the ideal end-states towards which the *processes* of interest in this account are seen to converge. So how does the liberal market democratic system work, in terms of it being both transformative and efficient? First, how has its quite distinct pluralism contributed to its success?

## The Role of Pluralism

Pluralism here means distributed discretion to act, and it is at the core of many accounts of progress. Its influence was noted early with the observation by David Hume in 1758 that political fragmentation had been the main reason behind Europe's beneficial flourishing of useful knowledge, noting the contrast at that time with China's loss of scientific momentum. Mokyr (2002) concluded that – without the pressure of competing neighbours – states sometimes lose their cutting edge. Confirming Hume, Mokyr (2017: 291) also pointed to an important difference in how markets for ideas worked. In the early 1700s in China, which was under centralized control, both allocative efficiency and market integration 'did not lag significantly behind Europe'. But a century later, Europe's contrasting political fragmentation had evolved to provide a set of political authorities that were mutually restraining and 'gave nonconformist thinkers in Europe substantial degrees of freedom'. As a result, there grew in Europe a 'Republic of Letters' inside which intellectual discourse could be conducted free of direct state control. New thinking had been decentralized.

New idealists could 'game the political system to avoid persecution' (Mokyr 2017: 171). By the closing decades of the eighteenth century, after much intellectual exchange, debate, and consensus-finding, 'the forces of the Enlightenment had become too powerful to resist'. Supporting this, Eric Jones's (1961) study of 'the European miracle' confirmed its most crucial determinant as the flourishing of independent centres.

The same avoidance of central monopoly power was clearly designed into the US Constitution of 1776. In this, a great deal of what is needed to regulate the daily life of citizens is decided not by central government but by the legislatures of the eventual fifty regional states. At this level, local interests and perspectives are given voice and their views can be factored into forms of order; so too is central state policy an outcome of majority agreement. Another version of this in Britain is the autonomy, over many matters, not just of the English parliament but those of Wales, Scotland, and Northern Ireland – and at another level much independence in cities. Other European states found parallel ways of avoiding the standardizing effects of a central monopolizing of influence. I once made the mistake in Germany, when teaching an executive programme for Mercedes Benz, of referring to the German system of employee participation. I was corrected immediately by a factory engineer who said, 'For us it is not German, it is Swabian'. So too did the CEO of Volkswagen (VW) once explain to me the great attractiveness to VW of the deep technical skills accumulated in the region around their Skoda partner in the Czech Republic.

The European Enlightenment over some centuries crucially brought with it a respect for rational thinking based on information. This attitude – along with Christian ethics – came to be absorbed into the world of commerce, in what was later celebrated by Weber (1930) as 'the Protestant ethic', included in which was a 'distinct and peculiar rationalism' (26), in other terms Adam Smith's 'invisible hand'. This would come to underpin market decision-making and allow an escape from the reliance on personalism that had acted as an invisible web of influences before then. As the ideals of the Enlightenment spread, there was a supportive spread of moral civic consciousness, the 'bourgeois virtues' described in detail by Deidre McCloskey (2016). New ideas over time dismantled old class systems. The seeds were sown of what later grew into the equality enacted in democracy.

Local spontaneously evolved new forms of rational order would find ways of working together in the wider European economy. This brought rising productivity in the use of assets, the full flourishing of which would run throughout the nineteenth century. Between 1600 and 1870, Europe's percentage share of world GDP rose from 17.1 to 30.5. China's declined from 29 to 17.1 and continued to fall to 3.1 by 1973 (Maddison 2007: 381). Devolved rationality and political fragmentation had long been at work across Europe. The US system of devolved power brought a similarly liberating, but still nationally integrated, outcome. Europe's own integration has maintained much national autonomy, with progress benefitting (with occasional lapses) from habits of 'enlightened' debate and behaviour and restraints on aggression. The preservation of national autonomy has been perhaps stimulated recently by the United Kingdom's separation in its pursuit of that fundamental principle.

## How Liberal Market Capitalism Evolved

The nature of liberal market capitalism derives largely from Enlightenment influences. As noted earlier in discussing transformation, it also benefitted historically from new access to resources and markets brought by colonial expansion. Seeing it as a system shared across several societies, initially Britain and the Netherlands, the main influences that shaped it have been individual empowerment, scientific rationality, and ethical ideals contributing to civically conscious behaviour – Heilbroner's (1985) 'more benevolent form of domination'.

Its local interpretations evolved further over the nineteenth and twentieth centuries as the first Industrial Revolution came to be carried so prosperously by the instruments of organizing made possible under the applied rationalities, conditioned as they were by the ethics of the Enlightenment that, for instance, opposed African slavery throughout the eighteenth century[10] and for Britain brought it legally to an end in 1807 (Biggar 2023).

The principal instrument for economic growth became the joint-stock limited liability company, which opened access to the crucial catalyst of secure private rights of ownership. This was also designed to be accountable to open scrutiny, accessible to investors, competitive in judgeable performance, and visibly rational in its use of resources. It came to be used by a new middle class which itself evolved to display high levels of the 'bourgeois virtues' that secured respect (McCloskey 2006, 2010, 2016).

A significant outcome became the capacity of the business world itself to take part in the creation of the surrounding institutions which could support its own workings. Typical outcomes were professions such as accounting and surveying, systems of banking and commercial law, and standardized forms of commercial dealings. These were fostered by social bodies such as Chambers of Commerce and industry associations protecting the business interests within the

---

[10] For example, the first volume of Tobias Smollett's novel *Roderick Random* in 1748 and the second volume in 1771 were influential and widely popular tracts against slavery, informed as they were by his experiences in the West Indies as a naval surgeon and his marrying into the Lascelles family who owned plantations in Jamaica (Brahm and Rosenhaft 2022).

wider societal processes. Their effect was to reduce uncertainty by providing reliable order. What would become known as 'civil society' was constructed from within itself. As noted earlier when discussing emergent order, an interpretation of this offered by DeLong (2022: 448) is the 'crowdsourcing' of legitimate societal order. In this process, certain responsible citizens are charged by the society's leadership with responsibility for coordinating a key aspect of a society's workings, usually within a city, trade, or profession.

A revealing illustration of this historical inventing of order is found in the history of London's guilds and the example of the Worshipful Company of Coopers, established by King Edward ll in 1307.[11] Making barrels in the fourteenth century was a critical skill, ensuring the safe distribution of liquids throughout the city. The work of the guild was to ensure the craftsmanship in barrel-making that guaranteed their safety as containers but additionally for the guild's wardens to maintain regular inspections of all the city's barrels to make sure the liquids in them were not being switched for different usages and so polluting the second liquid. For centuries, the Coopers guild used its right to issue fines for non-compliance. It taught apprentice coopers the skills to become masters of a craft, and its wardens also checked barrel use in the city's warehouses (Jackson 1914). In 1441, Thomas Willis was fined three shillings for being 'delinquent against the Tenor and Art of Coopers', and John Mertyn was fined ten shillings for 'vilifying the Wardens against the form and tenor of the City'. Six centuries on, the Coopers guild still has its own Livery Hall in the City of London and maintains two schools. Its motto remains 'Love as brethren'. The point of this anecdote is to show that – after delegation from the monarch – the society itself would take care of its needs for predictable order using institutions accountable for their conduct, even with love.

Over time, there emerged many other societal processes of communicative action that carried the new interflow of knowledge and opinion between people of business, scientists and other scholars, financiers, and local political figures. Typical of such networks in England were the Freemasons, the Literary and Philosophical Societies in the cities, and the many private dining groups such as the Lunar Society in Birmingham. These fostered the free exchange of ideas and pursued improvements in their fields of knowledge and practice. Another typical industry-based version is the Royal Smithfield Club, in London since 1798, whose members are market traders in meat but who brought scientific stimulus to many improvements in agriculture. The interests of the working class would later also become a focus of new social movements, inspired by the

---

[11] The tradition is alive and well and the Worshipful Company of Management Consultants was established in 1993 with similar core responsibilities and Royal Charter, as had been that of the Coopers six centuries earlier.

popular and realist work of writers such as Dickens in Britain, Balzac in France, and Mark Twain in the United States and of social theory by Karl Marx writing in the British Museum Library.

In building these stabilizing mechanisms, the European bourgeoisie was expressing the freedom to design itself to be informed, organized, collaborative, and efficient. So too was its moral foundation crucial for its long-lasting legitimacy. Such processes may be seen as manifestations of the deeper ideal of ethical self-expression, and so of balance. As the World Values Surveys show, that ideal evolved into action at this high level of independence only in Western Europe and its extensions. Its political expression is in democracy, with eventually full participation. Its early mediaeval moral core was Catholic asceticism (Baumard 2016) but with later additions further north under Protestantism. As explained by Max Weber (1930), such ideals underlay the 'spirit of capitalism'. But there was also the crucial practicality of 'communicative action' celebrated by Habermas (1984) as the primary way of delivering a society's capacity to transform itself towards what would become the 'modern'.

The central driving logics of the liberal market form of capitalism have then been the application of rationality within societal conduct, together with a benevolent form of domination founded in religious ethics. Rationality has two main effects: in the economy, it raises the efficiency of resource allocation and use; in society more broadly, it helps to reduce uncertainty and, by encouraging knowledge, critical thinking, and debate, to enrich the meaning of morality. These key issues have been discussed by Pinker (2021: 325–7) in explaining the rise of wealth. As he sees it, for most of human history 90 per cent of people lived in extreme poverty. Now only 9 per cent do. The great material enrichment of the nineteenth century was powered by energy capture, machines, and new financial technologies. But the new energy could not have been converted into widespread prosperity without legitimate societal systems to enforce contracts, within an ideal of civic duty to minimize aggression and fraud, and invest in infrastructure, research, and universal education. Democracy also served to reduce the chances of war and since 1945 has underpinned the work of the UN.

International trade added the stimulus of new resource access. New international organizations would evolve to reduce disputes. As to the influence of rationality on morality, Pinker suggests that the influence is indirect. Moral systems rest not so much on logic per se but rather on the acquired habit of considering the quality of moral arguments. Such moral propositions may have first been made centuries ago, as in religions, but can remain unimpeachable to a discriminating mind today, as, for instance, on slavery, war, or 'all you need is love'. In a more recent interpretation relevant to the theme of this Element, Pinker (2021: 325) implies that all you need is learning:

'Progress' is shorthand for a set of pushbacks and victories wrung out of an unforgiving universe and is a phenomenon that needs to be explained. The explanation is rationality. When humans set themselves the goal of improving the welfare of their fellows ... and they apply their ingenuity in institutions that pool it with others', they occasionally succeed. When they retain the successes and take note of the failures, the benefits can accumulate, and we call the big picture progress'.

Along with learning and ethics, the supporting processes in the *inspiring context* included 'empowerment', the process that revolutionized industrial productivity by releasing human brainpower in facilitating the best use of people's skills. Over time, and as technical complexity rose, the practice of management would come to be as much about motivation as about control (Drucker 1954). This released great new energies. So too did the open political debates encourage the support for working people that became the welfare state, as well as the newly significant influence of trades unions. This latter adaptation illustrates a further key process supporting transformation – the balancing of interests.

After this broad summary of the origins of the liberal market form, we now consider more specifically the three main clusters of processes which formed it: those making possible the society's (1) inspiration, (2) transformation, and (3) empowered action.

## Inspiration: Liberal Market Capitalism

At the apex of the proposed model of societal processes is an inspiring ideal, commonly seen as the most crucial role and responsibility of political leadership. Issues surrounding it include the perceived benevolence of authority, empowerment, freely reasoned critical thinking, and the maintaining of societal balance.

Matthew Arnold (1869) observed, in the middle of the first Industrial Revolution, that the modernization impulses released by the growing mastery of technology were changing the nature of society fundamentally and that this would challenge its cohesion. He advocated a new 'culture', the sharing of a renewed idea of societal perfection. Without that, the alternative was anarchy. A great deal of rich debate on this was then taking place nationally and internationally. This extended the prior 'Enlightenment' tradition of improving benevolence within the exercise of authority. Describing this subsequent adjustment, Heffer (2013) gave credit to the 'high minds' of the Victorian thinkers. McCloskey's (2006) celebration of the role played by the 'bourgeois virtues' is also apposite here. In the United States, parallel new thinking was equally changing society, with much new policy from lessons learnt in the Civil War.

A distinctly British reflection on Arnold's challenge for leadership to be *morally inspirational* so as to build societal cohesion was recently visible at the funeral of Queen Elizabeth II in 2022. The immense, unanimous, spontaneously disciplined – and totally silent – respect for her as a symbol of selfless virtue left a deep impression on more people than her own subjects. The distinct nature of a monarchy as a moral symbol above a democracy is perhaps an accident of history but its primary function of inspiring togetherness, by defining and representing honour and duty, remains an object lesson within the wide variety of political responses to that challenge found globally.

A theme emerges: it has been primarily the stable – and humanly meaningful – redistribution of authority that has led to the various successful forms of capitalism. This 'empowerment' takes precedence over all other factors in determining the capacity for the kind of progress earlier defined. When a society's habits reflect a concern for its members, then they in turn can see their membership as being part of a system that is at least aiming towards a shared ideal. Over time, from the world of Charles Dickens in the boot-blacking factory to the invention of the welfare state half a century later, the ethics of benevolence grew more significant as a unifying and motivating force. Across the many societies in the liberal market category in Europe, North America, and elsewhere, supportive changes were running in parallel. Formalized career training allowed individuals more options, and education fostered critical thinking; electoral reforms provided people with a voice; and prosperity itself brought its own form of energy through optimism. As noted, the attractions of this to many in other societies continue to justify the instinct of people to vote with their feet and migrate to it.

Alongside authority, and in many ways a consequence of it, is another factor within the inspiring context: the freedom of people to think for themselves and the ease of exchanging and debating ideas openly. This openness to knowledge and opinion, and escape from dependence on the minds of others (Kant's enlightenment), added greatly, although not always visibly, to the quality of thinking and creativity that societies became capable of. The process also boosted self-respect. In democracies, the quality of thinking is on constant public display and critique in two arenas: open debate in social settings, including a free press, and access to more sophisticated understanding through education. In consequence, the level of debate in democracies – in terms of quality of argument, evidence, and articulacy – has remained at a comparatively high level.

In governing, virtually all societies based on liberal market democracy create their laws in legislative assemblies working with open methods of debate, elected mandates, critical public comment, and the seeking of consensus.

Crucial to this system's success is one simple overriding mechanism: its legitimacy is regularly tested. A government needs to perform to people's satisfaction or lose its mandate. Above all other influences that simple performance discipline underpins the system's capacity to represent and so to create an inspiring context of societal encouragement. The 'liberal' nature of such processes is also visible in their capacity to tolerate varied interpretations of the ideal, most visibly in delegating much control to subunits in the system and not over-controlling the pluralism that results. As noted earlier when discussing societal order, much can be 'crowdsourced' to respected bodies, and that order is more likely to be appropriate to needs, safely embedded, and effective.

Evidence on the eventual outcome from applying ideals of freedom in this way comes from the global surveys of the Cato Institute, whose 2021 report is based on 82 indicators of freedom across 165 countries. Its findings are that the regions with the highest levels of freedom are North America, Western Europe, and Oceania. In terms of per capita wealth, there is a strong correlation between prosperity and democracy (Vasquez et al. 2021). The top quartile in the Human Freedom Index of 2021 had per capita income averaging US$48,748, and the lowest quartile US$11,259.

Another related source of inspiration within the liberal market condition is the neutral discipline of rationally assessed competition in open markets. This presents an overall non-negotiable, unavoidable, apolitical, and depersonalized logic that drives the search for productivity in the use of resources and brings market sensitivity in dealing with demand. Such objective logics are then built into organizational behaviour and surrounding regulatory frameworks. By bringing acceptable clarity across a wide range of decision-making, this also contributes to the capacity to absorb growing complexity in the economy, its technology, and its financing.

The liberal market form of authority is then in its design principles (its heart) – benevolent, trusting, and disciplined. It is also in large measure self-regulating, since – under the constant internal critique of its workings – it is under permanent review. This is not to say that it is faultless but that it is self-correcting. Some of its more visible shortcomings in recent years have derived from its being abused by (often external) actors exercising 'extraction' practised elsewhere and wishing to hide their wealth, only some of which becomes exposed. And in some Western societies, new forms of mass communication have – by weakening the objectivity of much information – brought out the excesses of special interest claims and given them strident voice. Predicted by Hayek (1979: 172), this force can become insidious if permissiveness based on biased or weak logic comes to the support of those claiming a share of societal wealth without their submitting to the discipline on which it rests.

## Transformation: Liberal Market Capitalism

In the liberal market case, the driving forces of free-market competition, transparent performance logics, and safe ownership of assets permitted entrepreneurship to flourish. This generated a flow of investment capital to support innovation and business venturing. Societies were transformed in many senses. In the economy, new forms of reliable, ethical order emerged, guided by the professions. Technology change in such fields as transport, healthcare, and manufacturing would improve living standards and life expectancy. For the typical society in this category, a common denominator was also the opening up of access to global commerce, the transformative power of which was celebrated in the great exhibitions referred to in the Introduction. Transformation was equally visible in other aspects of innovation and especially in the sciences, both natural and social. Work such as Darwin's *Origin of Species* inspired new standards of analysis. New universities were founded and technical inventiveness became self-perpetuating.

The transforming of society also saw a redistributing of influence within it. New means of cooperating evolved in the joint-stock enterprise. In DeLong's (2022: 1) account, the significant practical catalysts for the post-1870 growth were (a) globalization, (b) the industrial research lab, and (c) the modern corporation. Each of these could by then rely on faster access to better information. Social change began with new ideas about class, enfranchisement, and access to knowledge through education. It would see the invention of the welfare state and the rise of labour representation in national politics. In such ways, these societies, with their stable achievement of widespread consent, were able to adjust themselves to the possibilities and challenges of modern complexity and to change competitively while retaining a balance of interests.

## Empowered Action: Liberal Market Capitalism

Three processes in particular came to affect how the typical liberal market society in practice achieved the volume and quality of action on which its wealth came to be based. The first of these derived from the empowerment that came with the devolving of political influence into the society and the lessening of poverty. This downward sharing of influence fostered the growth of a bourgeoisie that – in liberating but ethical circumstances – would achieve a reputation for honourable civic behaviour, hence the 'bourgeois virtues' (McCloskey 2006). The growth of a civically conscious middle class gave rise to an entire series of new interactions that drove societal progress forward.

Identified by Habermas (1984) as 'communicative action', many of the social processes that drove these enhancements involved the emergence, and exercise of, social capital in committee rooms, at dining tables, and in board meetings. The concept itself is important in allowing an understanding of the catalytic effect possible when the personal perceptions within the 'lifeworlds' of individuals interact with institutions seen at the societal level.[12] As Habermas's (1984) translator McCarthy (1984: xxx) summarizes:

> The two levels are interconnected. Systemic mechanisms have to be anchored in the lifeworld, that is, institutionalized. More specifically, the rationalization of the lifeworld – particularly of law and morality – is a necessary condition for the institutionalization of new mechanisms of system integration – in the modern era, of formally organized subsystems of purposive-rational economic and administrative action.

So, economic modernization was approached through processes of interaction and exchange that brought together the meaning-systems of individuals in business with the surrounding world of societal responses in building new order. This worked fruitfully in the various cases of free-market capitalism and in some hybrids. Why it has not yet done so elsewhere is one of the main questions at the centre of this Element. Behind that wide question come three others to be carried forward:

(1) Is a particular society's lifeworld amenable to adjustment?
(2) Is there an encouragement for its influence to contribute to the societal response?
(3) Could adjustments to the society's institutional responses be as productive in facilitating efficient cooperation as those seen elsewhere if there is a mismatch between the lifeworld and an imposed response?

As the influence of social capital grew, the new forms of order and cooperation would provide the human networks over which the economy could flourish. In the words of Habermas (cited in McCarthy 1984: xxvi; emphasis in original): 'Under the functional aspect of *reaching understanding* communicative action serves the transmission and renewal of cultural knowledge; under the aspect of *coordinating action,* it serves social integration and the establishment of group solidarity; under the aspect of *socialization,* it serves the formation of personal identities.' As explained earlier from West (2017) on the growth of cities, the power laws of fractal geometry could then come into play as social interactions proliferated, thus yielding *returns* to scale to add to the *economies* of scale.

What has been distinct about the free-market form of society, in terms of empowered action, is that the key actors responsible for investing in, and

---

[12] A lifeworld is how the world is collectively perceived within a society: the socially constructed realities.

managing much of, the socio-economy became the shapers of its evolving structure. Being close to 'the action', they were building what was needed to keep the action moving, and for the good of all. In his recent study of the early history of the English merchants community, Edmond Smith (2021) describes how – by 1650 – with shared commercial experiences, education, and partici-pation in corporations, there had emerged a common culture and a regularity of beliefs, norms, and organizational practices. As their trading expanded globally, 'they continued to depend on the institutions that they had honed and developed over the preceding century which had helped to forge the networks of trust, credit and information that were so important for profitable international trade' (227). The outsourcing of order worked.

Such responsible engagement with societal progress is celebrated by Pinker (2018), who observes that earlier aristocratic, religious, and martial cultures, which had for centuries looked down on commerce as tawdry, were gradually replaced from the eighteenth century in England and the Netherlands by respect for the spirit of commerce with its ability to dissolve sectarian hatreds. A new praxis emerged in which were included 'norms of propriety, thrift, and self-restraint, an orientation toward the future rather than the past, and a conferral of dignity and prestige on merchants and inventors rather than just on soldiers, priests and courtiers' (84). As Pinker points out, the British nation of shop-keepers would by Napoleon's time be earning 83 per cent more than Frenchmen and enjoying a third more calories. Under the US version of the same ideal, its per capita GDP would grow from about US$3,000 in 1800 to about US$55,000 in 2010, with the UK's reaching about US$40,000 (Pinker 2018: 85). The world average had by then grown to around US$16,000, with that of China only loosely understood but perhaps US$12,000.

Describing the historical breakthrough in Britain, the United States, and the Netherlands as 'the Great Escape', Pinker (2018) notes that it was quickly followed by similar 'escapes' in the German states, the Nordic countries, and Britain's colonial offshoots in Australia, New Zealand, and Canada. Certain other non-Western societies would catch up later on their own terms as well as what they learnt or invented, dramatically so in the case of Japan. After 1950, the Great Escape turned into the Great Convergence (Pinker 2018: 85). That converging worked in two ways. States came to share more features of overall order; and with globalization, entrepreneurs at ground level came to share more knowledge, information, risk, and benefits. Societies were learning about the newly converging efficiencies, brought by information access, to cooperation and cohesion.

It is, however, necessary to note a counter-trend of special relevance to China's evolution from now on. This is a 'decoupling', especially between the

United States and China, as – in the light of new geopolitical frictions – they seek to lessen their dependence on each other as export markets (Witt et al. 2023). Consistent with the aim of escaping from dependence on the supply side, China's parallel Belt and Road Initiative is designed to secure crucial inputs long term. So, globalization is changing, as earlier dependencies fracture and new alignments emerge. The question of interest then becomes: will such rising independence foster world-competitive levels of productivity using technologies, institutions, and ideals that are not themselves still derivative? Can China inspire a new kind of human century?

## 7 The State-Directed Form: China

There are many versions of the state-directed economy in the categories of the global study by Witt et al. (2018) cited in the previous section. The case of China is seen within the category of *emerging economies* and – given that it ranks second globally in GDP size – it is taken as our main example of the wider state-directed type. The general tendencies that go with such political domination are reported as displaying 'high level consistency' across the *emerging* category (Witt et al. 2018: 26). Such features and implications are shared – although not directly replicated – for instance in Russia, Indonesia, Venezuela, Brazil, much of Africa, and most of the Middle East. The main shared features are: weak past and current general education; short-term job tenures; private skills acquisition; suppressed unions; bank-led finance allocated on the basis of relationships and state guidance; top-down decision-making inside firms, with low delegation and promotion based on relationships; family and state ownership of firms with often poor investor protection; low rule of law; predatory state policies; top-down state decision-making with generally low levels of voice and accountability; and overall poor state effectiveness. Most emerging state-directed forms of socio-economy have, in other words, not yet changed from central control to stable widely empowered influence and initiative. Attempts at DeLong's 'crowdsourcing' of emergent order have been handicapped.

A sobering reflection on this overall challenge has been offered recently by Subramanian and Felman (2022a, 2022b) in an examination of how state policies in the hybrid case of India in recent years have been so biased towards the support of national champions in industry that the side effects have included resistance by potential foreign direct investment (FDI) entrants and slow overall growth. Typical symptoms include the perceived risks of unstable incentive policies; the reversing of allowances; the favoured national champions' resistance to partnering; tariff costs of entry; weakening access to low-cost trainable labour; and national macro-economic imbalances. India's large indigenous informal private sector has also had its momentum slowed by new forms of taxation on goods and services. Subramanian and Felman's view is that recent growth has been at around 2.5 per cent per annum as opposed to the 7 per cent seen as potential.

So, the question of order keeps returning. How might a society encourage legitimate stable order to evolve in the hands of ethically responsible actors who themselves deal directly with the task of bringing such order to the accumulating complexity?

## China's Evolutionary Path

China's core ideology is described by Fairbank et al. (1965: 82) as follows: 'In her own tradition, China was, and always had been, in the centre of the civilized world, surrounded by peoples of lesser culture who invariably acknowledged the cultural superiority of *Chung-kuo*, the Central Country.' This ideology has tended to be communicated from the centre in 'sacred' claims. In this view of itself – doubtless well-founded in the pre-modern era when it evolved – China's order and harmony were taken to be closer – than in 'barbarian' lands – to the natural order of the cosmos, with stability based on proper conduct specified over key relationships, status, and hierarchy. A scholarly mandarin class administered the state on behalf of the emperor. Extended family responsibility for welfare was based on particularist ethics of personal conduct rather than on the universalist demands of legal regulations, religious principles, or market logics. Personal advancement rested on self-cultivation, and especially through learning the Confucian classics. The intended – and long achieved – aim was stable hierarchical order.

For most of China's history, economic life was a combination of family-based agriculture, local craftsmanship, and limited-scale commercial trading. This was a pre-industrial form of society in which, as Elvin (1973) noted, commerce substituted for management. Agriculture was predominantly small-scale. Local buying and selling was more significant an activity than was large-scale manufacturing, processing, and wider distribution. Society was designed to be hyperstable as long as everyone behaved according to the rules, and roles. Further complexity would require state control. Such intentions excluded influential public opinion, widespread empowerment, or radical spontaneous change, nor would these features be later brought by Marxism, which contains no formulae for encouraging the commerce that might support them (Popper 1962). Instead – despite its egalitarian claims – the state simply redefined its ideological source of dominance (Brandt and Rawski 2022). The effects of this are still visible at ground level in the continued response for order to be based on the ethics of interpersonal reciprocity. Given the consequently limited integration, Shambaugh (2013) has judged the outcome as a 'moral void' tolerated by a people brought up to play a zero-sum game against others; the overall result being a 'partial power' with limited social capital. Today's attempted correction of that by the state-regulated compliance disciplines of the Social Credit Index implies an acknowledgement of the void. That index might yet prove to be – for a culture accustomed to obedience – a viable means for diffusing new ideals of civic obligation.

From a study of the social origins of state development over Chinese history from 618 to 1911, Wang (2022) explains further the 'partial power' outcome. He compares China's use of authority with that evolving over the same period in Europe.[13] As he explains the contrast, China's rulers were both constrained by and reshaping (when they had the opportunity) the elite social terrain to achieve a trade-off between state strength and their personal survival. In contrast, the many separate European states had increased their capacity to collect taxes, and by the modern era they had become more benevolently integrated and stronger, whereas the Chinese state had gained stability at the expense of state strength.

The paradox in Chinese history is that, by the emperor's skill in dividing and overpowering the society's elites, personal imperial *rule* endured but the *state* itself would, in a repeating pattern over centuries, lose strength. As Wang's data indicate, 'The trend of ruler duration is in stark contrast with that of state strength, starting with the decline in fiscal capacity over the Song era' (Wang 2022: 54). This trend within reigns towards fiscal weakness was evident in the contribution to GDP from taxation over the 200 years prior to 1900: in China, it averaged less than 2 per cent, while in the UK it rose from 11 per cent to 19 per cent. The endings of reigns also kept revealing tensions within the elite. Between 221 BCE and 1912 CE, there were 282 emperors. Half of these exited office unnaturally and of these half were deposed by the elite (Wang 2022: 53).

Wang (2022: 57) also identifies three long phases of equilibrium in the history of China's state development. The first from 618 to 907 he terms 'State Strengthening under Oligarchy', in which the ruler had the benefit of high state capacity but at the expense of personal power. For these three centuries, it was the set of powerful oligarchs within a strongly centralized state who provided national stability until climate shocks led to rebellions in the tenth century.

The longest equilibrium was built from 960 to 1840 as a form of 'State-Society Partnership' in which the influence of social elites came under the close

---

[13] For a confirming account of much longer and deeper historical determinants of the same contrast, see Welzel (2013).

control of a scholarly mandarin civil service. The resulting absolute monarchy dominating a now fragmented and localized elite came eventually to rule at the expense of a much-weakened state, which had by then resorted to outsourcing much public goods provision via local lineage organizations. In the pre-industrial context of agriculture plus mainly local commerce, this deeply conservative form of collaboration lasted up to its eventual interaction with influences from a newly modernizing and industrializing external world.

The subsequent more punctuated equilibrium from 1840 to 1911 is termed by Wang 'State Weakening under Warlordism' and was initiated by the Opium Wars and the conceding of the treaty ports. Over the second half of the nineteenth century, given the rise of private militias and the Taiping Rebellion, the central state lost its ability to protect its citizens from violence. Control by the mandarinate faded away, and that reduced the influence of the remaining central elite until dynastic rule fell in 1911, leading China into a twentieth century of severe and often damaging turbulence, wars, and revolutions.

Comparing China with Europe brings to the fore again the crucial issue of state size and indivisibility. Over the same period just considered for China – and following the 'Dark Ages' at the end of the Roman Empire – Europe's trajectory from the seventh to the twentieth century began with a legacy of many small kingdoms. Local rulers and their attached elites came to directly control many aspects of society and resources. The elites were given titles and centuries of land ownership in exchange for their cooperation in taxation and war. Local assemblies, including 'free' cities, were encouraged to deal with regional affairs and interests. These partnerships lasted throughout the mediaeval period and were only weakened when new military technology raised the cost of state defence or expansion, as, for instance, to build navies from the seventeenth century onwards. Feudal power then became more centralized but by then supplemented by both professional bureaucracies and standing armies.

Over centuries, the central function of the European monarchies was either dissolved or adapted away from absolute influence to symbolic representation of the wider public good. New ideals of citizenship evolved; and new assemblies were institutionalized, with much power devolved. The commercial class became engaged as responsible contributors and participants, expressing the bourgeois virtues described in McCloskey's theory of progress. As Wang sees it, nation-states in Europe steamed ahead.

As the 'European miracle' was explained by Jones (1981), it grew out of the competitive but cooperative vitality of different societies. Under an overarching set of essentially Christian cultural fundamentals, as well as a great deal of peaceful commercial interchange, entrepreneurship was able to vary in practical application and would consequently encourage specialisms appreciated within the wider market. For instance, linen came from Ireland, tweed came from Scotland, and silk came from Lyon (Finlay 2021). The latter had its own 'Inspector of Silk Manufacture', and it was where its industry had learnt so much from the dobby loom that had been acquired there from China in 1601 – a borrowing that suggests respect for China's early capacity for technical innovation.[14]

The main contrast between Europe and China historically has then been in how authority was structured to provide both social stability and progress. Europe saw its separate states grow steadily in strength. As Greif (2006: 210) explains, religious controls on family membership in mediaeval Europe had brought a concentration on nuclear families and a consequent reduction in the role of wider kinship groups. To fill the vacuum in forms of societal coordination, one key response was the rise of the voluntary, public, self-governing corporation. This in turn encouraged property rights, public goods, new forms of order, markets, innovation, and training, with the state providing overall security. It encouraged what Greif sees as a particularly European institutional foundation of markets, polities, and knowledge.

China, as a single monolithic imperial state, regularly struggled with the balancing of stability and economic growth. Its immense size has always been both a blessing and a handicap to the decentralization of authority. As noted, there was a period in Chinese history when a long-lasting balance of influences was achieved under the mandarinate, even though this was at the long-run cost of much imposed conformity. As Wang (2022: 58) observes, 'social scientists who write about China's state-building process have not paid enough attention to this long period of state-society partnership'. But, as he also suggests, Chinese rulers have always faced 'the sovereign's dilemma', a fundamental trade-off between state control and state effectiveness. The dilemma was that a coherent elite seeking change that could collectively strengthen the state could also overthrow the ruler. The dilemma exists because the two demands of (1) strengthening state capacity while (2) keeping rulers in power for longer required different, and potentially contending, social networks – regional and central – in which the elites were embedded.

A form of the 'sovereign's dilemma' applies currently when civic consciousness has become subject to close surveillance and where forms of 'consultative authoritarianism' across both government and industry bring all dealings under close ideological control. In this tense context, a temporary experiment with

---

[14]  Much detail on the history of China's societal capacity is in Joseph Needham's (1956) extended studies of science and civilization in China.

decentralization during the Deng opening after 1980 produced a great surge of growth, but subsequent accounts have described the 'diminishing space' (Yuen 2015) of civil society and the return of the centralized norm (Teets 2013; Youwei 2015).

As noted in discussing the role of water dependency on societal responses, such instinctive centralization of control is argued by Welzel (2013) to be anciently rooted in the national culture as rational response embedded since the time of the civilization's ancient ecologies. Reliance on the centre has persisted, and so too the relative non-empowerment of the population. Constraints on freedom are made more tolerable by familistic identity as the alternative to dependence on the state. This biases societal cohesion towards the interpersonal bonding that remains the cement of Chinese society. Integration then rests on particular reciprocities and patronage dependencies. Evidence from Drew and Kriz (2014) shows that, even when exercised in mixed-culture environments outside China, the reliance on *guanxi-based* bonding is retained, although it also adapts to new surrounding structures, where, for example, education in or collaboration with other cultural influences can expose people to alternative ideals.

Such *guanxi* networks have proven to be a uniquely powerful basis for cooperation, especially in Asian regional contexts outside China where such alliances have been able to work harmoniously with market-rational bureau-cratic structures of ownership and control and merit-based forms of respect. But what happens without the rationalizing influences available within such hybrids? We are reminded by Commander and Estrin (2022) that the link between business and politics in Asia overall occurs within a 'connections world' and that its personal reciprocities and patronage ties can still impede the *full workings* of sustainable economic and political systems. It may have worked in some industries, and some societies, but it comes with significant costs and fallibilities. For the current case of China, notable tensions are huge market power but the attenuation of competition; threats to the growth of productivity and innovation; corrupt acquisition of assets; very heavy debt – state and private; and massive inequalities that challenge political stability (Ang 2020). In China, the overall picture on inspiration remains one of tension between the needs for control and for creative innovation. To hold together a sixth of the world's population is a formidable achievement. To take it forward with a legitimate 'China Dream' is an even more formidable challenge in a fast-changing world where many competing cultures work on the basis of differently achieved balances of power.

The essence of China's imbalance is economic. As Pettis (2022) explains, China has grown in recent decades, with its industry coming increasingly under state control. This has separated it from most global norms for the use of capital. Investment as a percentage of GDP in mature economies ranges from 17 to 23 per cent, and in developing economies from 28 to 32 per cent. For a decade, China's has been between 40 and 50 per cent. To reduce that would now bring a sharp downturn in overall economic activity. When seen as debt, China's official debt ratio has risen since 2008 from 150 per cent to 280 per cent of GDP – 'one of the fastest increases any country has ever experienced'. This rise has been carried mainly by private investment in property, as well as often grandiose local government investments in infrastructure. In consequence, non-productive investment has come to account for more than half of all GDP growth and has now led to a clampdown on leverage in a situation where real estate prices have been higher than the comparable US level. Pettis concludes that there is no evidence that China will manage a rebalancing of the distribution of income that other countries with similar problems have been unable to achieve.

A tension then remains between the hierarchy's duty for societal control at the world's greatest scale of land and population and the need to foster transformation in a changing world. Authority in China remains party-based and all-pervasive and policy debate is restricted. The temporary relaxing of these restrictions in the period of opening up under Deng Xiaoping after1980 led to a burst of new energy that saw the national GDP (at PPP) rise from 3 per cent of the world's total to 18 per cent by 2018.[15] Trade in goods between the United States and China exploded from less than $8 billion in 1986 to more than $578 billion by 2016 (Campbell and Ratner 2018). But central control has now returned, in part responding to the coronavirus threat but also in part to avoid societal fragmentation, as, for instance, that based on traditional regional identities.

Over the period from 1950 to 2016, world GDP grew 4.4 times. Considering only growth and ignoring initial size, the GDP of the United States grew 3.5 times, China's grew 16.3 times, and Taiwan's 30 times.[16] A warning by *The Economist* (2023) sees planners in many governments unprepared to admit a looming crisis in national budgets, as public debt levels rise to new heights.

For China itself, in the post-1980 period of great growth there was a pattern of steady rise but a more recent slowdown. According to Bloomberg, the average rate of real GDP growth in China over the seven decades from the 1960s to the 2020s has been at the following percentages: 4, 6, 9, 10, 11, 7, 4.[17] Many analysts of such phenomena ascribe the slowdown to the effect of the middle-income trap

---

[15] International Monetary Fund (IMF), CRS Reports, *World Economic Outlook* (2019) China.

[16] Our World in Data, Maddison Project Database 2020: ourworldindata.org/.

[17] Bloomberg Terminal WRGDCHIN.

(Eichengreen et al. 2011), noted in considering societal transformative capacity, as the test of a state's capacity to adjust to the inexorable complexities of modernization.

Escaping that trap has relied elsewhere on the stable achievement of empowerment in ways that release new creative energies and inventive action. Responses can then deal with the challenges and opportunities of the increasing complexity brought globally by new technology, communications, and knowledge. In this, a society's processes need to meet the demands for balanced transformative capacity as the world changes. This requires the stable sharing of both thinking and authority. Without such resilience being built into the microprocesses at ground level, centralized responses to the rising complexities are handicapped. Most developing societies are still unprepared to meet this invisible middle-income transition, which is why it is a trap.

Like China, many countries find ways of absorbing the *techniques* that are parts of the requirement, as, for instance, through education, technology transfer, joint-venturing, or intellectual property acquisition. But as noted from Ferguson (2011), what are less transferable are new attitudes to the sharing of authority and of discretion to decide. Instead, in China top-down control has been asserted more firmly.

China's state-owned enterprises are managed mainly through a central body, the State-owned Assets Supervision and Administration Commission of the State Council (SASAC), which overlooks the state's investment interests in industry. In 2005, the state sector accounted for 47 per cent of industrial profits, while the private sector share was 13 per cent, with 28 per cent foreign. A surge of the private sector then followed the 2008 financial crisis and – aided by policies of opening up – the private ownership share grew to 40 per cent by 2016. As to efficiency, the state sector's return on assets has declined over the last decade from 3.5 per cent to 2 per cent, while the private sector's rose from 3.5 per cent to 4 per cent. On other criteria, the private sector now accounts for 60 per cent of GDP, 70 per cent of innovation, 80 per cent of urban employment, 90 per cent of new jobs, 70 per cent of investment, and 90 per cent of exports (Zitelmann 2019). China's capitalism is no longer state-dominated in any complete sense because private sector management remains so significant, but the latter has now become state-influenced, since all private companies have party committees to oversee compliance. The state is also capable of influencing both state and private sector power to serve political aims, as has been made clear in the takeover of Hong Kong (Kwok and Patterson 2022). The overall type is now more properly party-state-industry.

But Deng Xiaoping's surge is still remembered, and we now consider how China might attempt to regain its competitiveness against the many external business systems built on the different basis of the crowdsourcing of innovation described by DeLong. We first consider the processes within the *inspirational context*, before looking at China's other two sets of societal processes, those of *transformative capacity* and *empowered action*.

## China: An Inspiring Context?

In China, a quite distinct set of societal processes contribute to its *inspirational context*. Empowerment and critical thinking take on forms quite different from those found in the liberal market contexts. A new study of the China response by Yeling Tan (2022) shows how three major bodies of influence have been interacting over recent decades: the central party authorities, the regional party powers, and the external World Trade Organization (WTO). Each of these has a distinct policy-driving ideal, and the interplay of these ideals has not been at all straightforward. The tensions between them persist.

The account by Tan is based on the content analysis of a large body of government documents and her findings are summarized as follows:

(1) From an external perspective, the agreement by China to join the WTO was a matter of learning to play by the rules of law in global relations and business. This perspective did not much overlap with Chinese ideals, within which is an assumption of building its own form of strategic competitiveness.

(2) The external assumptions did not allow for the nature of China's authority traditions, or its habit of experimental, incremental change.

(3) Within China, two party bodies came into contention over policy. The central party group came to promote a form of state capitalism as the key platform in a 'developmental' model influenced by the technical standards and law reforms for which they were responsible when dealing directly with WTO. Differently, a subnational party group came to promote a more 'directive' policy towards the industries they had influence over, especially regionally. This latter response evolved in conditions where regional officials were not directly accountable for dealings with WTO but were nevertheless directly exposed to the pressures of foreign competition. These two overall policy positions – the nationally 'developmental' and the locally 'directive' – have been out of alignment.

(4) In the quest for FDI, the ideals were also in conflict. Central party policy would maximize incoming technology to boost industrial sophistication, as, for instance, with semi-conductors and automobiles. Local party policy would instead seek to boost incoming investment capital and lower-level industry such as assembly and testing. Over time, the local preferences came to dominate, and R&D nationally was relatively disadvantaged.

(5) The growth of globalization has tended to add legitimacy to the state capitalism formula, but the WTO has not reduced its suspicions of that formula and the intentions behind it. International tensions have consequently increased and are currently visible in the US policy of non-cooperation in fields involving advanced intellectual property.[18]

(6) Tensions have also remained endemic within China between the centre and periphery, and an underlying contrast in aims remains unresolved, other than by the vertical assertion of power.

The effects of these local–central and China–WTO tensions over policy are visible in results. In the thirty years from 1950 to 1980, China's economy grew at a relatively low annual rate from 900 billion to 1,700 billion (in PPP US$ value). That period had included the Great Leap Forward and the Cultural Revolution. New thinking after Mao's death in 1976 eventually led, under Deng Xiaoping, to the opening of the economy to external influences. New policies emerged: special economic zones, stock exchanges, overseas stock listings, entry to WTO, inward foreign investment, investment in science, Belt and Road Initiative, the re-possession of Hong Kong, and 'Made in China' policies for 2025 and 2035. Between 1980 and 2020, China's economy grew ten times from $1,700 billion to $17,000 billion.

It is necessary to acknowledge that this massive growth in prosperity, seen by Ang (2020) as China's 'gilded age', had included within it 'vast corruption'. Such corruption took four forms: *petty theft* by non-elites; *speed money* to grease the palms of officials holding permission rights; *grand theft* by political elites as with embezzlement or misappropriation of large sums of public money; and *access money* paid by business leaders to powerful officials for access to exclusive, valuable privileges.

But, as Ang (2020) explains, the seeming paradox that corruption in China coincided with growth leads to questions about the moral framework within which cooperation occurs. Her data show that access money was its predominant form, and the possibility arises that this was a rational response to deal with the weakness of other forms of coordinating action surrounding investment and risk. 'Although access money poses long-term economic risks and undermines the CCP's legitimacy, it does not deter private investment and business activities in the short term' (51). The study also showed that in different societies processes of corruption take different forms, with different effects, and so – as with drugs – not all corruption harms in the same way. In rankings of most or least overall corruption, out of fifteen countries China comes ninth, with

---

[18] The CHIPS and Science Act of 2022 is designed by the United States specifically to limit technology access by China, whether by buying in or organized collaboration.

Russia second, India seventh, Japan thirteenth, the United States fourteenth, and Singapore fifteenth.

Recent adjustments by Beijing have added wider surveillance and more extensive control via party committees in all companies, local and foreign. The context has reverted to greater control. We now consider the issue most related to that: the question of transformation.

## China: Transformative Capacity

The key processes that build a society's transformative capacity are innovativeness and adaptiveness. The first of these relates to invention itself, and so is mainly visible in the world of science and technology. The most common indicator of this is the registration of patents. In China, activity on this increased dramatically after 2000. But patents registered are not patents subsequently granted, and those granted in China were 23 per cent of those originally registered, compared to 44 per cent in Germany, 45 per cent in the United States, 46 per cent in South Korea, and 50 per cent in Japan. The subsequent classification of patents granted defines them as 'invention', 'utility', or 'design'. China's 'invention' patents were 19 per cent of those granted (or 4.37 per cent of those initially registered). A Federal Reserve Bank study concluded that 'the actual technological improvement in China is not significant compared with the skyrocketing number of patent applications' (Santacreu and Zhu 2018: 2). A further indicator of patent quality is registration abroad, since that indicates value needing protection: here, China registered 6.31 per cent of its patents, whereas the US figure was 48.1 per cent.

In their study of China's innovation challenge, Lewin et al. (2016) saw China as having high absorptive capacity and clear aspiration to great power status. They also noted the significance of the great size of its market and of its available workforce in science and technology. But, citing Chen et al. (2015), they also acknowledged a weakness affecting the society's transformative capacity. This affects the practical application of *indigenous* new scientific research and it stems from (1) unclear protection of intellectual property, (2) not enough quality research with commercial relevance, and (3) inadequate support for venture capital start-ups.

In a new study of learning and innovation in Chinese firms, Hong and Li (2023) present a more positive view, seeing China as now an emerging innovation economy. In this, they suggest that the phase of 'duplicative imitation' is now evolving towards a new era of 'accelerated or novel innovation'. This change has been driven in part by a series of government policies designed to bring it about.[19] At the same time, there appear reports that question progress in strengthening the context of creative openness. The Academic Freedom Index (based in Berlin) currently scores China 8 out of 100, with others being: United States 90, United Kingdom 92, Sweden 96, South Korea 87, Taiwan 87, and Russia 37.[20] For China, this suggests a still weak connection between a key source of free thought and societal transformation.

Related to that is a significant emergent issue in information technology: the Chip War (Miller 2022). The context of that is full of tension because the technology to produce the new forms of microchip uses extreme ultra-violet lithography. At the far limit of this technology is that developed by the Dutch company ASML, now discussing transistor nodes at three billionths of a metre and subject to quantum effects at the subatomic level. In terms of influence, a powerful grouping has emerged whereby the coalition of ASML, TSMC, Samsung, and Intel supplies other firms with their needs. No one else can currently make such chips. Miller suggests that China is consequently facing its 'Sputnik moment', as did the United States in the mid-1950s. Crucial in all this now is the US (and more broadly Western) policy to ban microchip exports to China.

From 1980 to 2010, China did achieve a massive transformation with a great display of innovative strength. This was driven from the centre by the vision of Deng Xiaoping to embrace aspects of world trading practices that would permit administrative and productive fusion between its factories and the markets of the world. In a fine-grained study of this transformation, Chung and Hamilton (2009) explain how a new hybrid form of capitalism emerged from that fusion of inherited norms with external forms of organizing. What evolved was not so much a paradox as a conscious blending: a socio-economic example of the principle of *yin-yang* balancing by a collaboration of opposites, expressed in Deng's initial exhortation during his legendary Tour of the South: to 'Point to the left, then turn right'.

As Chung and Hamilton summarize events, the prior form of business system that had evolved in China in the early 1900s had been mainly (but not entirely) in private hands. That earlier system was 'profoundly commercial', a point echoing tradition as described in Mark Elvin's (1973) history of Chinese business. Described by Chan (1977) as based on the interactions of merchants and mandarins, it was essentially mercantile capitalism based on buying and

---

[19] Examples are the Medium to Long-Term Plan for Science and Technology Development; Made in China 2025; the National Hi-Tech R&D Program; the Double First-Class University Plan in education.

[20] Academic Freedom Index, Berlin, Global Public Policy Institute. gppi.net.

selling, as opposed to 'industrial' capitalism where value is added by the transforming of goods inside a firm for wide marketing.

Up to the late nineteenth century, China's international trade was controlled, and key goods manufacture was under state control. The rest was regional buying and selling. As Chung and Hamilton (2009: 55) note, 'Commerce was largely self-regulated by merchant groups, and the organizational tools they used to control commerce were regional and occupational identities. These bodies would establish business rules and conditions of trade, and they held monopoly power over who could engage in business.' There were rules to control business size, numbers of branches, and profits distribution. Associations within a trade would resolve disputes and they would also act like mini clearing houses to preserve the group's trading monopoly. Order was then effectively being crowdsourced.

This traditional Chinese economy was based more on cooperation than on competition. Its world of connections was a long way from alternative disciplines of open free-market competition. The system more or less survived through the upheavals of the first half of the twentieth century but was then suddenly transformed in 1949 under Mao. The party then took over the economy, removed most of its supporting fabric and appropriated the assets of the 'landlord' middle class. Deng's post-1980 reforms would later redress some of the human disasters that had resulted[21] and would release a flood of new investment, and of internationally linked institutions, to connect China with world markets.

In that post-1980 period of rebuilding, there was also a discrete but influential force – the bridging of two worlds by the ethnic Chinese in the countries around the South China Sea (Redding 1990). The *Nanyang huachiao* numbered approximately 100 million people who had long lived inside the WTO world but retained an instinctive identity with Chinese civilization. Creators of one of the world's most effective business systems, usually owned in family-based structures, the 'Overseas Chinese' had mostly left China to escape poverty during various phases of its late nineteenth- and twentieth-century history (Chan 1977). Many of them settled in the West, but the majority moved into the nearby countries to the south. First inspired by intellectuals such as Sun Yat-sen and then later by leaders such as Chiang Kai-shek and Lee Kuan Yew, they settled into the world of global business in Taiwan and also places which – by accidents of history – were under British, Dutch, or French administration, and American interest.

---

[21] Estimates reported by Dikotter (2010) are of 45 million deaths in the great famine of 1958–63 and a further 2 million over the Cultural Revolution between 1966 and 1976.

This distinct system of capitalism came to have a significant role in the evolving of societal progress in China itself. The workings of this catalyst are visible in the network-building that carried much of the integration of China's economy into those of the wider region to the south (Redding 1990, 1995) and later the world. Externally, the great interchange centres were Hong Kong and Singapore, as they became global cities, but also Taipei, Manila, Jakarta, Bangkok, and Saigon – so too their strong presence in San Francisco, Vancouver, and so on. Historically bonded through mercantile trading on the *nam-pak-hong* (north-south company) networks, the interchanges would grow to include more industrial investment as China's growth picked up over the 1980s. By 2000, the Overseas Chinese had become the major external investors in the economy of China.

As well as bringing in capital to China, significant intangible assets were included, especially those that could facilitate China's fitting in to the global systems overseen by the WTO. Some of the resulting standardization would take place in higher education, as with MBAs, engineering degrees, and legal and accounting qualifications, but much would also be absorbed within the new international joint-venture companies that acted as conduits into China for techniques designed to match global performance standards in marketing, design, technology, and production efficiency. Acknowledging the above facts of history as catalysts of transformation during the twentieth century, we now return to consider China's trajectory of progress in the light of the wider set of societal processes shown in Figure 1.

As noted by *The Economist* (2022), China has for four decades defied received wisdom about making countries rich, since its market reforms were not followed by matching political reforms. Instead, the politics of control has continued via the co-opting of local power brokers, such as regional and clan leaders and village elders. In the period between 1990 and 2010, much of the annual growth in emerging economies was led by China under the Deng Xiaoping reforms. In China, growth has since declined to the world average.

Aspects of significant societal transformation in addition to scientifically invented new products tend to be new forms of order and related institutions. For China, with its low civic consciousness and the retained dependence on family and personal networks, social capital in its modern guise is weak by international standards. The bourgeoisie that re-emerged after 1980 under the Deng reforms has since then necessarily adjusted to further party control. There are consequently fewer independent vehicles of complex integration, outside those of the state, to carry new initiatives forward. At the same time, party approval and supervision present a formidable obstacle to spontaneous change at any level. For China to achieve high levels of *transformative capacity*, it would benefit from adjusting its processes of both *inspiration* and *empowered action*. We now consider that last key to progress.

## China: Empowered Action

The empowering of action in any society comes about through the workings of three processes. The first of these – communicative action – has been discussed in relation to the application in practice of the principle of critical thinking. The second aspect is spontaneous ordering, as, for instance, when 'crowd-sourced' in trading or co-investing. Here are worked-out improved systems for facilitating the interactions. These can result in new ways of stabilizing connections, as, for instance, with standard documentation and ways of keeping accounts, norms for employing staff, and so on. At another level, they may work to influence standards within an industry, as via forms of association such as Chambers of Commerce.

Such processes of cooperation can build structures in a society that reduce uncertainty and foster trust. The resulting groupings within the wider 'civil society' then protect the general integrity and cohesion of part of the society such as a trade or profession and the 'reliability' effect spreads more widely. The responsibility for this stabilizing process varies societally between the state and the societal members. In the case of China, party control of societal order is such that any administrative system will inevitably be closely monitored and controlled. This does not remove the risk of changes stemming from wider socio-economic conditions of the kind most easily detectable by the key actors themselves, as, for instance, when skilled labour is no longer available or when an industry's mode of operating is changed by new technology. But if these are not picked up by government, adaptation may be slower and/or less sensitive than it might have been.

Globally, the fundamental contrast between the empowered and the disempowered forms of society ultimately correlates with most of the differences in societal progress so far (Polanyi 1944; North 2005; McCloskey 2016; Mokyr 2017; Pinker 2018; Mazzucato 2021; Fukuyama 2022). Without releasing the creative responsiveness of key actors in the socio-economy, no society can respond adequately to the rising societal complexity that all societies increasingly face. China's version of civil society has long had its own family-focussed special nature. Ethics of reciprocity provide means of outreach to non-family others, but the sense of civic consciousness now being built rests not so much on a traditional ideology but on a mechanism of surveillance. Spontaneity in such emergent ordering is likely to be inhibited under such oversight. Nor might order feel 'owned' by its users. Chinese competitive productivity in the world of business has a long and distinguished history both internationally and in conducive conditions in China such as those between 1980 and 2010. But with a base of co-opting political support, and so of hierarchical dependence, the system would predictably lose resilience, a phenomenon also visible in another low-trust state: Russia.[22]

## 8 Lessons from the Comparisons

The performance comparisons allow us now to assess the liberal market-driven and the party-state developmental socio-economic forms in terms of the one feature above all others that can best assure fitness for progress in any such complex adaptive systems: their transformative capacity. The significance of such resilience has also risen as the world faces newly pervasive and more threatening change: great powers conflicts such as China versus the United States and Russia versus Europe; giant debt leading to inflation; pandemics; turbulence in key resource markets; and internal conflicts of left versus right populism in developed democracies. Above all these are the major changes in information technology and the explosion of communications but with a related rise of uncertainty over content reliability. The overall impression is of new hazards, at higher scale, with a more fractured understanding of their import.

It is not surprising that Jeremy Rifkin (2009), in a sweeping history of civilization, concluded by defining an inevitable tension between human empathy and system entropy. Resolving this tension is the critical test of the species' ability to survive and flourish. This requires resilience based on an ethic of empathy, in which good-quality knowledge then takes on even greater significance. For such resilience to be deployed effectively, it requires a careful balancing of the many forces within the society, such forces including assets available in different forms but under the pressures of possibly disparate interests: capital and labour, state and private, local and foreign, socialist or liberal, perceived exploiters or victims.

Comparison begins by being specific about the two main approaches. One approach is inspired by thinkers such as Hayek and Schumpeter and sees progress as resting on the market-driven creative destruction that generates constant adaptation to produce wealth competitively and to distribute it rationally for related performance. The second approach is associated with thinkers such as Polanyi, whose view was that land, labour, and finance could never be removed from a society's moral and religious underpinnings; and if they were,

---

[22] Russia is not discussed here but a recent confirming account is available in Libman and Obydenkova (2021).

such influences would still subtly intervene in the economy's workings. Keeping the story to its essentials, one can follow DeLong's (2022: 168) 'principal grand narrative' that it was John Maynard Keynes who brought the two approaches together and fostered the capacity in some societies to balance and protect both the private and the public interests. This fusion was effective enough to allow recovery from the 1930s Depression and the Second World War. It did so in the United States, in DeLong's words: 'like a shotgun marriage in which Hayek and Polanyi awkwardly kept house under social democracy for decades – as long as the country was blessed with Keynes's full employment – more inclusively than before, and with sufficient, if wary, cordiality' (411).

It could be argued that a new process of restoring balance is now evolving rapidly in the market-driven Western case. This is visible in the call for a switch away from a form of capitalism biased towards shareholders to a capitalism rebuilt around the interests of 'stakeholders'. This is, for instance, argued by Fortune's CEO Alan Murray as 'tomorrow's capitalism', his theme being that of a new search for 'the soul of business'. This theme would fit into what is termed here (see Figure 1) the 'inspiring context', achieved via the balanced orchestration of the forces of transformation and empowered action. Seen at the level of the firm, the outcome of any such achievement would be that 'capitalism 2.0 would be more human, more conscious, more creative, more compassionate, more inclusive, more focused on creating shared value, more dedicated to solving the problems of people and the planet' (Murray and Whitney 2022: 211).

In order to explore further DeLong's (2022) significant conclusion that the successful long century ended in 2010 as the Western formula began to suffer the inadequacies that go with it, two insights will be brought to bear on the nature of the evolved tensions that now underlie the West's recent loss of balance. The first of these reflects Hayek's instinct that the releasing of too much freedom could be dangerous for the cohesion of a civilization. The second comes from the (initially financial) imbalances that result from the threatening combination of a neoliberal turn and hyper-globalization. Still respecting their gravity, they will be graphically labelled (in my terms) the *squeaky wheel effect* and the *shotgun marriage outcome*.

## The Squeaky Wheel Effect

In popular parlance, the squeaky wheel gets the most grease. In free and open societies, it is possible for distortions to evolve whereby those who make the noisiest claims on a society's resources end up receiving disproportionate benefits when seen in the wider context of perceived fairness. This effect is boosted by the amount of media exposure now available to such claimants in this age of hyper-information. Along with this goes an enfeebled quality of debate about fundamental societal priorities, often subliminally fed by residual Marxism and/or postcolonial adjustments. Historically, there are strong grounds for arguing that the redistribution of societal wealth has been a necessary achievement in any trajectory that improves a civilization's quality. So, discourse on redistribution has often been under the ethical banner of 'rights'. That deepest principle is not at issue. What is at issue is whether a civilization's ideals of fairness, including its understanding of 'rights', are themselves becoming unbalanced by a technological innovation in communications and a paradoxical weakening in the quality (as opposed to the amount) of critical thinking.

Seen by Hayek (1979: 172) – in a view judged by DeLong (2022: 93) as 'absolutely essential in making sense of the long twentieth century's economic history' – the new permissiveness 'assisted by scientistic psychology has come to the support of those who claim a share in the wealth of our society without submitting to the discipline to which it is due'. DeLong (2022: 535) himself poses the wider question: 'Why, with such godlike powers to command nature and organize ourselves, have we done so little to build a truly human world, to approach within sight of any of our utopias?' To consider that question further, I turn now to the tension between the Western and Chinese theory camps that represent the alternative broad approaches to societal progress. In doing so, note will be taken of how any relationship between them may prove fragile. I will conclude by revisiting the main themes that run through this Element.

## The Shotgun Marriage Outcome

In a comment on the general tension between the market logics of efficiency and the social logics of fair distribution, DeLong (2022: 529) considers that the shotgun marriage that produced the post–Second World War social democracies was 'as good as we have so far gotten'; but it has begun to fail its own sustainability test. Decades of rapid growth have brought high expectations but 'Polanyian rights required stability, the treating of equals equally, and the treating of perceived unequals unequally in ways that neither the Hayekian-Schumpeterian market economy of creative destruction nor the Polanyian social democratic society of universal egalitarian social insurance rights could ever deliver' (529).

As noted from Bresser-Pereira (2017) and echoed in the above clarion call by Murray, there is now a consequent need to widen and enrich the definition of what capitalism is for. In DeLong's (2022) account of that issue in the Western case, the new tensions derive from five forces:

(1) From 1990, Germany and Japan began to challenge the technical leadership, and the exceptionalism, of the United States.
(2) Forms of fanatic religious violence reappeared in several areas.
(3) A Great Recession began in 2008.
(4) Global warming began to show its early effects.
(5) China's potential for resurgence showed signs of being shaped not by a new ideal of utopia but instead by another cycle of rulers and ruled, with 'the strong grabbing what they wished and the weak suffering what they must' (531).

In the context of such globally relevant tensions, Mariana Mazzucato (2021) argues for a restructuring of contemporary capitalism. Directed principally at the liberal market form, the principles she expresses nevertheless have wider relevance. 'Public purpose must lie at the centre of how wealth is created collectively to bring stronger alignment between value creation and value redistribution . . . to re-imagine what type of society we want to build, and the capabilities and capacities we need to get us there' (Mazzucato 2021: 7–8). The related advice includes dynamic capabilities in organizations; outcomes-based financing; shared risks and rewards in distribution; purpose and stakeholder value-sharing in partnerships; and open systems participation for co-designing intentions.

Mazzucato illustrates this potential approach by referring to the major rethinking in the German Bauhaus period after 1919, and in Roosevelt's New Deal of the 1930s. Her emphasis on agreed outcomes, shared intentions, and new ideas consistently points to the crucial nature of what is seen as the capstone in this Element: a society's *inspiring context*. Whether that is termed a society's heart or its soul, the essence is the same: that the society maximizes the moral potentialities of its people and does so in a way that each person can become conscious of making a respected contribution, can know the difference between good and evil, and can help make the society empathetic, harmonious, peaceful, creative, and supportive (Hacker 2021).

At the global level, much recent discussion has been about the 'decoupling' of established connections, as the structures of industry, finance, and governance are realigned to deal with threats from the major totalitarian states, and while the logics of the middle-income trap become more pressing in many other states where resilience is constrained by an ideology of power.

In a study of the function of freedom in evolution, Bejan (2020: 51) concludes, in relation to societies, that there is 'a continuation of the natural order of things that happen by themselves, and which have empowered western society to this day: work ethic, philanthropy, merit system, speaking truth to power, rule of law, change, hierarchy, and above all freedom'. He further observes that:

'With freedom comes evolution, and with evolution come all these visible things, complexity, diversity, hierarchy, size, and seemingly free choices that speak of the universality of economies of scale . . . Evolution can be predicted by invoking the law of physics that governs the evolutionary phenomenon' (109).

Another theorist of societal progress sees one particular link still challenging theory as 'the gorilla in the room' – the insufficiently studied knowledge-based legitimizing of authority (Mokyr 2009). An ancient model of this was the Chinese mandarinate, its symbolism adopted by the 'Whitehall mandarins' of the British public service. But the role of cultivated intellect in administration as underpinning the security of moral purpose in a government remains an issue that needs more up-to-date understanding in a fast-changing world and also relates to the pinnacle of the explanatory model in Figure 1 – the political capacity for inspirational ethical leadership as the basis for orchestrating the balance of societal processes and the countering of extraction.

There are already significant theories about a key transitional stage in progress as a society comes to terms with the increasing complexity it faces. At its simplest, this entails the transition from a pre-modern condition to a modern one while retaining the moral and societal supports that see the process as legitimate. If a society fails to adequately think through the challenges of such adaptation, it may see its growth level off and possibly decline relative to others. The tensions that usually arise at this stage tend to be subtle, opaque, and unfamiliar. The outcomes associated with such tensions are seen from different theoretical perspectives: Cardwell's law on the stifling of technical progress by government control (Cardwell 1972); Solow's (1994) 'residual' if technological change is treated as exogenous; North and colleagues' (2007) focus on necessary new institutions; the middle-income trap (Eichengreen et al. 2011); Kleiber's law of returns to scale (West 2017); the role of diffused autonomy (Fukuyama 2018); societal transformative capacity (Eisenstadt 1965); the role of empowerment (Pinker 2018); the role of knowledge (Mokyr 2002, 2009); and perhaps most fundamentally the role of virtue (McCloskey 2006). So too is the including of all interests now adopted as the banner for a movement among free-market thinkers towards 'stakeholder capitalism'. These theorists, and many others, have played a part in the thinking behind this Element. A summary of those challenges is proposed in simple form as four issues that need to be faced as any society progresses:

(1) The availability of freedom to change.
(2) The role of knowledge quality and access.
(3) Initiative acted out in entrepreneurship.
(4) The sustaining of a society's moral legitimacy.

## The Distribution of Authority and Freedom to Change

The most straightforward argument for the stable sharing of authority is that such a response correlates highly with societal and individual prosperity. In Bejan's (2020) conclusion on the role of freedom in progress, such empowerment is closely associated with access to learning. Distributed power to think and debate critically is then seen at the centre of a nexus of reciprocal influences. This includes the hierarchical speaking of truth to power. Without such exchange about understandings and principles, certain processes are handicapped: the motivating power of benevolent authority is blocked; so too is critical thinking handicapped and communicative action and spontaneously created order are limited. The structures of order do not then evolve spontaneously in the fields of action. This is not to say that industry cannot proceed with relatively disempowered personnel. It is instead to say that only a limited set of industries can compete globally using those features. Hence the transitory nature of the 'workshop of the world' phenomenon.

What we then observe in the more prosperous forms of capitalism studied is a correlation between devolved freedom and the transformative capacity of the societal system as a whole. In contrast, centralized authority in China (and also Russia) prevents both the emergence of a form of domination perceived as benevolent and the exercise of freely reasoned and informed critical discourse. Without these processes at work, transformative capacity is handicapped (except in extraction). Innovativeness in science is comparatively weak, even though small-scale entrepreneurial innovation, and opportunistic extraction, may remain. Cooperativeness is constrained by endemic mistrust and by subjugation to systems of limited access. The balancing of interests under top-down control proceeds with weak inputs from below. Economic action occurs under close scrutiny, which in turn inhibits the spontaneous inventing of new forms of response. Competitive productivity remains positively influenced by global market rationalities, but their influence may diminish, as it has for instance under China's plans for 'dual circulation' (Paterson 2021) in which its focus turns to more reliance on domestic market demand and the protection of state interest.

In the case of free-market democratic capitalism, authority is decentralized in both the economy and the polity. Freedom to change is unfettered and change itself is high on the public agenda in much discussion – both formal and informal. Entrepreneurship is enabled at high intensity by its established legitimacy, its supporting infrastructures, its perceived virtue, its competition-based productivity, and its positive contribution to equitable societal good. High levels of technical inventiveness are part of the societal context. Freedoms exist of many kinds but within systems of order that maintain stability and openness. These can become stressed when opposing forces are firm, but given widespread public oversight, entrepreneurship will normally prevail eventually. Resilience is part of the fabric.

Although the Western category contains several societies, such as those in the EU and Australia, which achieve different states of balance, their formulae tend to be democratically evolved and locally legitimate without running counter to the overall ideals of freedom and civic identity within the wider remit under discussion.

For the hybrid case of Singapore,[23] freedom is high in the economy, although somewhat more subject to conformity in the public context. This is consistent with the cultural heritage and so is seen as legitimate. A high penetration of global influences has added other stimuli for freedom, especially in the roles of law, public voice, and institutional order. The atmosphere of progressive change stays alive and well in this open society with its ideology of meritocracy.

The fundamental philosophy of the free-market form has never been better expressed than by John Stuart Mill (1859) in his study of the principle of liberty. At the centre of his account are two core ideals defining the appropriate use of power in a society. The first is that individual rights of independence over people's own bodies and minds is absolute. 'No society in which these liberties are not, on the whole, respected, is free, whatever the form of government' (21). This freedom gives people the option of uniting in a cause, but for that another principle comes into play. This second principle is that: 'the only purpose for which power can be rightfully exercised over any member of a civilized community against his [*sic*] will, is to prevent harm to others' (17). His reasoning being: 'Mankind are greater gainers by suffering each other to live as seems good to themselves, than by compelling each to live as seems good to the rest' (21).

In further justifying such individual freedom, Mill states that:

> It is not by wearing down into uniformity all that is individual in themselves, but by cultivating it and calling it forth, within the limits imposed by the rights and interests of others, that human beings become a noble and beautiful object of contemplation; and as the works partake of the character of those who do them, by the same process human life also becomes rich, diversified, and animating, furnishing more abundant aliment to high thoughts and elevated feelings, and strengthening the tie which binds every individual . . . . by making the society better worth belonging to, each person becomes more valuable to himself, and is therefore capable of being more valuable to others. (91)

---

[23] For an explanation of Singapore's 'meritocracy', see Wooldridge (2021).

There are few more convincing summaries than that to represent a version of the apex of the explanatory model proposed here: the *inspiring context* for which a society's leadership is responsible. Writing in the middle of the nineteenth century, Mill also observed many cases of societies in which doctrine is imposed and 'the creed remains as it were outside the mind, incrusting and petrifying it against all other influences addressed to the higher parts of our nature; manifesting its power by not suffering any fresh and living conviction to get in, but itself doing nothing for the mind or the heart, except standing sentinel over them to keep them vacant' (487). This then points to the question of a society's knowledge, Mokyr's 'gorilla in the room'.

## The Role of Knowledge

Most societies pay tribute to the acquiring of knowledge through education. But the question in hand is about societal progress, and that is not only about *acquiring* knowledge but also about *using* it, especially when societal transformation is justified. In that case, it is reasonable to suggest that in the case of democratic free-market capitalism Western-style (and in the hybrid styles of high-performance capitalism represented by Japan, Singapore, and South Korea) knowledge takes on high significance and flourishes freely as an influence. Public knowledge is built on a high level of educational access. Freedom of discussion is high. There is an effective network of facilities in which to exchange ideas and debate them, even though there is an accumulating threat from the big-tech monopolizing of much information access. Such societies consequently evolve under a wide plebiscite of interested parties. Government is regularly legitimated. Competitive change in the economy is normal.

Russia and China share a different perspective on the use of knowledge. In both cases, although technical knowledge can reach high levels, the broader systems of societal understanding of the kind that might be relevant to change are controlled politically to varying degrees. Authority then stifles resilience.

## Entrepreneurial Action

When people are getting together to exchange and debate ideas, to perhaps then collaborate in future action and to remain active in a trusted network, such processes make the world of business go round. If actors can then collaborate further to improve their society's surrounding support structures, then the society builds capacity to further transform itself effectively. As Habermas described this integrating process, it works by people internalizing dominant values, renewing cultural knowledge, integrating socially, and forming personal identities. It becomes a powerful creator of social capital, and it is normal in the free-market capitalism form and the several hybrid forms. It is, however, handicapped in the various centralized forms. This is because it presents an alternative source of influence to that of the party/state, and networks might then persist in terms of ritual but will lose their autonomy over action. Initiatives for change may then become narrowly debated.

## Sustained Moral Legitimacy

For a socio-economy to flourish, it needs an inspirational and therefore fundamentally ethical purpose, an insight now at the heart of the Western movement to re-examine the 'soul of business'. This can help retain the 'hidden hand' rational processes to create wealth to be then shared with others. In the case of Western free-market capitalism, this was achieved by creating rewarded employment and then taxation to support a welfare state. Its main carrier was a bourgeoisie that came to be seen as virtuous: good employers and good citizens. Domination had evolved to be perceived as benevolent. Although its Western Enlightenment version is distinct, its inspiring nature had made it a respected form on the basis of what it delivered.

In China (and also Russia), the historical legacy has led now to systems of neo-patrimonialism that become conducive to rent-seeking and patron–client relations. The attendant risk of extraction and cynicism is high. The further effect of any extraction is to undermine the potential value of an inspirational ideal relevant to all contributors: entrepreneurs, business partners, investors, financiers, employees, customers. Social capital then returns to its instinctive base – the personalized reliabilities and predictabilities of small-network trust and family reciprocities. Limits to trust then constrain the integrity of the institutional cement holding together the fabric of society (Commander and Estrin 2022).

## Can an Autocracy Change?

The question of change is always relevant but especially now for the case of China, because of its great size and also given the progressive capacity it demonstrated in the 1980–2020 period of great growth. Related too is the economic power and experience of the regional ethnic Chinese in the field of business, including globally, and their loyalty to the ideal of China as the great central civilization. History also shows that certain Asian societies, steeped originally in the Confucian ideal of strong vertical control based on traditional scholarship, learnt to change under the realization that the global world brought new threats and opportunities. This transforming influence had perhaps its deepest effect in Japan but later also in South Korea and Taiwan and in other parts of Southeast Asia. The post-Confucian case of Japan will be briefly noted now for its great weight in the global arena, for its long evolution, and for its retaining of a clear national identity. It shows that very successful transition to the modern can occur when transformative capacity is available.

In 1601, the great shogun Tokugawa at the Battle of Sekigahara brought an end to a long period of warring fiefdoms and united the country. His reputation as the 'maker of modern Japan' (Sadler 1937) rests on what he then promulgated: a renewed form of society in which much authority was passed into local hands overseen by an intellectual caste of 'samurai' guardians of order. This first great rethinking owed much to scholars such as Ogyu Sorai and Ito Jinsai, and it led to the embedding of ideals of learning, filial piety, loyalty, and courage. In the transition as described by Yamashita (1996: 153), 'the government authorities found Confucian ethical discourse eminently useable ... and supplied a means for the state to cultivate willing subjects'. But crucially in this latter regard – and as an illustration of Japan's transformative capacity – the ethics texts were being continually revised from the outset.

Two crucial outcomes followed. A distinct and stable tradition of devolved power had been established under Confucian ideals. But it was conservative, and by the nineteenth century Japan was forced to realize its technological weakness. The long Tokugawa Shogunate came to an end when in 1868 Emperor Meiji took back the reins of power. He then in effect oversaw the transformation of Japan into its own version of a modern state, eventually capable of matching the West in industrial power and in prosperity. This was achieved in an extended process of learning from other societies how a modern state works. Commissions were set up, each specializing in a field of societal conduct – political structures, ways of business, employment norms, technology, education, social welfare, and more. These issues were studied in detail, with commissions visiting countries wherever best practice could be studied. Japan's systems of public administration and industrial support were then redesigned to apply what was learnt, with allowance for the cultural differences taken into account during their implementation. In consequence, Japanese industry would learn to become globally competitive while still retaining a distinct Japanese quality at its heart. The subtle essence of that quality remains tangible today in the high levels of work ethic, of order, and of worker participation in a typical factory.

The case of Japan shows that a transition from hierarchical Confucian tradition to the modern dissemination of freedom and responsibility is possible. Parallels could also be cited of similar transitions being achieved via different trajectories, as in South Korea's balancing of state and modern industry influences, in Singapore's meritocracy (Wooldridge 2021), or in Hong Kong's (until 1997) balanced blending of East and West. The keys to progress remain constant: knowledge and critical thinking about the options and their implications; transformative capacity; and retained benevolent domination. And there is no rule that says others have to be copied – just perhaps learnt from. Japan remains very much its own self.

## 9 Implications for an Unknown Future

It is not intended to deal here with questions about progress in specific societies but instead to concentrate on the fundamental insights of universal relevance that may then be interpreted and expressed by any society in its own way. So, the discussion now returns to the deeper lessons of history.

   To seek implications means to assume certain universal human instincts at work everywhere and that such instincts are relevant to forms of cooperation and of authority that come into play in generating societal prosperity anywhere. This then requires an understanding of the societal processes that enhance the instinctive collaboration between individuals, and so too the possibility of constant improvement in the productive use of such collaboration to the benefit of the society at large. What then are the most fundamental conditions that allow that transition to take place? How is rising complexity absorbed?

   Three effective principles of responses have been identified from the lessons of history to date. First, the thinking and action applied in adapting a society should be sufficiently diffused to permit those directly facing the new complexity to creatively take part in influencing the response to change. Second, the action taken should enlarge the public good and not undermine it. Third, the society should remain coherent and cooperative under a shared sense of belonging and morality that influences positively each person's identity and behaviour. As an example at large scale, the contrasting workings of such universal principles are visible in the differences now between Japan and China, both originally Confucian.

   The findings from many societies, and what lies behind them, were summarized in the set of ten conjectures about human progress to date – the 'lessons of history'. As such, they remain open to refutation on the basis either of new evidence or of irrelevance to a specific case. Until they are refuted or amended, they represent what has been widely learnt so far. Whether, and specifically how, they apply in one particular society is best tailored to that society's own constructed reality.

## Agendas for the Release or the Control of Human Energy

The questions to be posed now are about specific interpretations of the three overriding themes suggested as universally relevant for the large-scale stable cohesion of human groups: the diffusion of empowerment, focus on the public good, and societal coherence. Significantly, for the processes to be cohesive it is also assumed that a society will have an inspiring soul (or heart), whether openly acknowledged or not. Questions are addressed here to the two main stereotypes discussed: liberal market democratic and party-state-capitalist. To set the stage, it is first necessary to summarize the current status of each so as to focus on the differing challenges they face. The core dilemma of the liberal case is that of controlling the potentially disruptive tendencies within hyper-energized and opinionated societies. The core dilemma for the party-state case is to be able to encourage and release such energies productively while keeping the society stable.

*Liberal market democratic.* This form of socio-economy has achieved ascendancy over its history by balancing the eight key processes within the three themes in such a way that has released much human creative energy. Results have been: the ability to innovate technically; legitimated decentralized political power was influenced by widespread and informed opinion; and societal adjustments were able to keep pace with wider changes of many kinds. Knowledge grew via deep science and by vibrant, open, rationality-based debate. The system has, however, recently begun to suffer from political and economic instabilities that stem from (1) very high levels of technology innovation affecting communications, especially by growing their quantity but diluting their average quality; (2) the consequential rise of new claims to rights by many subgroup interests; (3) the political instability that results; and (4) shortfalls in visionary leadership capable of gathering enough legitimacy to match the new larger and more complex threats that accompany the globalizing of many issues and the high speed of technical innovation. The essential liberal dilemma is one of renewing inspiration to then permit the overall rebalancing and stabilizing of a basically very productive but now widely 'owned' formulae.

*Party-state-industry.* This form of socio-economy has evolved in the case of China out of a historical pattern of repeated attempts to reconcile the central control of order with the retention of productive creativity in the world's largest state, where the state's size itself brings the permanent challenge of manageability. A heritage of repeated failures to maintain stable productive growth suggests that the embedded instinct for centralized control tends to bring with it repeated discontinuities (Wang 2022), while the philosophical base of the culture has historically acknowledged the value of some lessening of the traditional central domination (de Bary 1957). China's current challenges include a slowing down of its recently liberated successful growth, new threats to its financial stability from a destabilizing of the property market and from state investments with poor returns, technology dependence, flights of both capital and talent, withdrawals of foreign investment, and an impending long-term threat from a decline in population reducing both labour availability and national revenue generation. Additional issues consequent to new global ambitions include a fracturing of established trading relationships. As to governance, there has been a return to strong central control via the Chinese Communist Party (CCP) and the extensive use of surveillance to ensure the orderly compliance of citizens with civic obligations. In broad terms, initiatives from the base face obstacles from state requirements for compliance.

## Key Challenges for Liberal Market Democracy

As suggested, the threats to continued progress for the liberal type of socio-economy stem from recent challenges to its long-standing formula for benevolent domination. These come from two main sources: new competition aided by its acquiring of transferable know-how (as opposed to knowledge) as industry goes global; and new internal pressures of entitlement fed by relatively uncontrolled new volumes of communication. Political clarity has been compromised by the resulting complexity, and governments suffer from enforced compromise, erratic responses, and a rise in public cynicism. Inspiration has been weakened.

## Questions for Liberal Market Democracy

(1) How can a society's 'dream' be reformulated to reinspire citizens? Can it reconfirm the ethically responsible ideals attached to entrepreneurship? Can it make better use of the informed critical thinking within industry and commerce?

(2) How can the idea of transformation be more strongly legitimized as part of the redefined ideals?

(3) How can acknowledgement of a society's 'heart' or 'soul' be folded into policymaking as an aspect of inspiration?

(4) How can the influence of new competing interests be rebalanced so that responses to them remain acceptable to the claimants?

(5) How can the full benefits of communicative action be preserved in the new conditions of communications technology?

(6) Are the people happy? Why or why not?

## Key Challenges for the Party-State-Industry Form in China

Here, the central issue is escape from the historical pattern of interrupted growth and the repeated state weakening associated with the tradition of central control. The resulting current conformity-based stability may inhibit spontaneous creativity. Order centrally imposed may be inadequately designed. Other factors adding complexity include population decline, large accumulated obligations of debt, rising competitor states, the weakening of labour-cost advantage, and rising non-cooperativeness internationally.

## Questions for the Party-State-Directed Form

(1) What may be learnt from earlier indigenous political theory about the balanced inclusion of freely constructed contributions to policymaking?

(2) How can Chinese pride in its own civilization be harnessed to support new applications of its great strengths in organizational coordination, in such ways that retain its long-standing reputation for moral conduct at globally understood standards?

(3) How can its internal cultural response of zero-sum attitudes, personalized dependencies, and low civil consciousness be recalibrated by incentives biased more towards encouragement than towards penalties?

(4) How can the long-standing traditions of industry guilds and associations be more fruitfully encouraged by their being given responsibilities for specific aspects of public order, with social respect being allocated when this process is virtuously conducted?

(5) Can depoliticized sources of societal information be enhanced?

(6) Are the people happy? Why or why not?

The complexity faced by societal leaders everywhere is now rising unpredictably under pressure from forces new to humanity. Understanding these challenges and coordinating stable responses that keep societies balanced, is an always-evolving capability that will inevitably lead to variety in responses, that variety being largely the product of each society's history and geography. Learning from the example of others is thus limited, but it is not impossible, if done with sensitivity and adaptiveness. In that learning process, one key condition is to understand certain human universals driving societal progress. As in the world of medicine the doctor does not blame or criticize, but helps people to deal with the human universals, so too in the world of societal development. This Element is designed with that intention.

A final thought on the fundamental and universal influences comes from Lemn Sissay (2022) – cited in the Introduction to represent the main lesson here – through his understanding of the idea that a society has a heart. Like the poet, this Element asks two ultimate questions of any society. Does it have a kind heart? Whose heart is it?

# References

Acemoglu, D., & Robinson, J. A. (2012). *Why Nations Fail: The Origins of Power, Prosperity and Poverty*. London: Profile Books.

Ang, Y. Y. (2020). *China's Gilded Age: The Paradox of Economic Boom and Vast Corruption*. Cambridge: Cambridge University Press.

Arnold, M. (1869). *Culture and Anarchy*. London: Cornhill Magazine.

Baumard, N. (2016). *The Origins of Fairness*. Oxford: Oxford University Press.

Bejan, A. (2020). *Freedom and Evolution: Hierarchy in Nature, Society, and Science*. Cham: Springer.

Berger, P. L., & Luckmann, T. (1966). *The Social Construction of Reality*. London: Penguin.

Bergsten, C. F. (2022). *The US vs China: The Quest for Global Economic Leadership*. New York: Columbia University Press.

Biggar, N. (2023). *Colonialism: A Moral Reckoning*. London: Collins.

Brahm, F., & Rosenhaft, E. (eds.) (2022). *Global Commerce and Economic Conscience in Europe 1700–1900: Distance and Entanglement*. Oxford: Oxford University Press.

Brandt, L., & Rawski, T. G. (2022). 'China's great boom as a historical process.' In D. Ma & R. Von Glahn (eds.), *The Cambridge Economic History of China*. Cambridge: Cambridge University Press, 775–828.

Bresser-Pereira, L. C. (2017). 'The two forms of capitalism: developmentalism and economic liberalism'. *Brazilian Journal of Political Economy*, 37(149), 680–703.

Campbell, K. M., & Ratner, E. (2018). 'The China reckoning: how China defied American expectations'. *Foreign Affairs*, March–April.

Cardwell, D. S. L. (1972). *Turning Points in Western Technology: A Study of Technology, Science and History*. New York: Science History Publications.

Chan, W. K. K. (1977). *Merchants, Mandarins and Modern Enterprise in Late Ch'ing China*. Cambridge, MA: Harvard University Press.

Chen, A. H., Patton, D., & Kenney, M. (2015). 'University technology transfer in China: a literature review and taxonomy'. *Journal of Technology Transfer*, 41(5), 2–39.

Chung, W. K., & Hamilton, G. G. (2009). 'Getting rich and staying connected: the organizational medium of Chinese capitalists'. *Journal of Contemporary China* 18(58), 47–67.

Coleman, J. (1990). *Foundations of Social Theory*. Cambridge, MA: Harvard University Press.

Commander, S. & Estrin, S. (2022). *The Connections World: The Future of Asian Capitalism*. Cambridge: Cambridge University Press.

De Bary, W. T. (1957). 'Chinese despotism and the Confucian ideal: a seventeenth-century view'. In J. K. Fairbank (ed.), *Chinese Thought and Institutions*. Chicago, IL: University of Chicago Press, 163–203.

DeLong, B. (2022). *Slouching Towards Utopia: An Economic History of the Twentieth Century*. New York: Basic Books.

Dikotter, F. (2010). *Mao's Great Famine*. London: Bloomsbury.

Drew, A., & Kriz, A. (2014). 'Institutional reform and the changing face of guanxi'. *International Journal of Business and Information* 9(2), 187–216.

Drucker, P. L. (1954). *The Practice of Management*. Cambridge MA: Harvard Business School Press.

*The Economist* (2022). 'A new chapter', 13 October, p. 58.

*The Economist* (2023). 'Stuck in fiscal fantasy land', 6 May, p. 9.

Eichengreen, B., Park, D., & Shin, K. (2011). 'When fast growing economies slow down: international evidence and implications for China'. Working Paper No. 16919, National Bureau of Economic Research, Cambridge, MA.

Eisenstadt, S. N. (1965). 'Transformation of social, political and cultural orders in modernization'. *American Sociological Review* 30(5), 659–73.

Elvin, M. (1973). *The Pattern of the Chinese Past*. Stanford, CA: Stanford University Press.

Fairbank, J. K., Reischauer, E. O., & Craig, A. M. (1965). *East Asia: The Modern Transformation*. Boston, MA: Houghton Mifflin.

Ferguson, N. (2011). *Civilization: The West and the Rest*. London: Penguin.

Finlay, V. (2021). *Fabric: The Hidden History of the Material World*. London: Profile Books.

Foster, G. M. (1967). 'Peasant society and the image of limited good'. In J. M. Potter, M. N. Diaz, & G. M. Foster (eds.), *Peasant Society*. Boston, MA: Little, Brown, pp. 300–23.

Frankopan, P. (2023). *The Earth Transformed: An Untold Story*. London: Bloomsbury.

Friedberg, A. L. (2022). *Getting anihC Wrong*. New York: Wiley.

Fukuyama, F. (2018). *Identity*. London: Profile Books.

Fukuyama, F. (2022). *Liberalism and Its Discontents*. London: Profile Books.

Gallup J. L., Sachs, J. D., & Mellinger, A. (1999). 'Geography and economic development'. Working Paper, Center for International Development, Harvard University, Cambridge, MA .

Galor, O. (2022). *The Journey of Humanity*. London: The Bodley Head.

Geertz, C. (1973). *The Interpretation of Cultures*. New York: Basic Books.

Goldthorpe, J. H. (2021). *Pioneers of Sociological Science: Statistical Foundations and the Theory of Action.* Cambridge: Cambridge University Press.

Greif, A. (2006). 'Family structure, institutions and growth: the origins and implications of Western corporations'. *American Economic Review* 96(2), 308–12.

Habermas, J. (1984). *The Theory of Communicative Action: Reason and the Rationalization of Society.* Boston, MA: Beacon Press.

Hacker, P. M. S. (2021). *The Moral Powers: A Study of Human Nature.* Hoboken, NJ: Wiley Blackwell.

Hayek, F. A. von (1979). *Law, Legislation and Legitimacy: The Political Order of a Free People.* Chicago, IL: University of Chicago Press.

Heffer, S. (2013). *High Minds: The Victorians and the Birth of Modern Britain.* London: Random House.

Heilbroner, R. (1985). *The Nature and Logic of Capitalism.* New York: Norton.

Hong, J., & Li, S. (2023). *Learning and Innovation of Chinese Firms.* Berlin: De Gruyter.

Hopf, T., & Allen, B. B. (2018). *Scientific Cosmology and International Orders.* Cambridge: Cambridge University Press.

Hume, D. (1758). *Essays and Treatises on Several Subjects.* London: A. Millar.

Inglehart, R. F., & Welzel, C. (2005). *Modernization, Cultural Change, and Democracy.* Cambridge: Cambridge University Press.

Inglehart, R. F. (2018). *Cultural Evolution.* Cambridge: Cambridge University Press.

Jackson, J. (1914). *Notes on the History and Antiquities of the Worshipful Company of Coopers.* London: Worshipful Company of Coopers.

Jones, E. L. (1981). *The European Miracle.* Cambridge: Cambridge University Press.

Keynes, J. M. (1933). *The Means to Prosperity.* London: Macmillan.

Koyama, M., & Rubin, J. (2022). *How the World Became Rich: The Historical Origins of Economic Growth.* Cambridge: Polity Press.

Kwok, D. W. H.x. & Patterson, J. (2022). 'Taiwan: a risk analysis through the lens of Hong Kong'. Policy Brief Research Paper, Ash Center, Harvard Kennedy School, May.

Lewin, A. Y., Kenney, M., & Murmann, J. P. (eds.) (2016). *China's Innovation Challenge: Overcoming the Middle Income Trap.* Cambridge: Cambridge University Press.

Lewis, W. A. (1954). 'Economic development with unlimited supplies of labour'. *The Manchester School Journal* 22, 139–92.

Libman, A., & Obydenkova, A. (2021). *Historical Legacies of Communism: Modern Politics, Society, and Economic Development.* Cambridge: Cambridge University Press.

Madden, B. J. (2020). *Value Creation Principles*. New York: Wiley.

Maddison, A. (2007). *Contours of the World Economy 1–2030 AD*. Oxford: Oxford University Press.

Mazzucato, M. (2021). *Mission Economy: A Moonshot Guide to Changing Capitalism*. London: Allen Lane.

McCarthy, T. (1984). 'Translator's introduction'. In J. Habermas, *The Theory of Communicative Action, Vol. 1: Reason and the Rationalisation of Society*. Boston, MA: Beacon Press, vii–xxxix.

McCarthy, T. (2009). *Race, Empire, and the Idea of Human Development*. Cambridge: Cambridge University Press.

McCloskey, D. N. (2006). *The Bourgeois Virtues: Ethics for an Age of Commerce*. Chicago, IL: University of Chicago Press.

McCloskey, D. N. (2010). *Bourgeois Dignity: Why Economics Can't Explain the Modern World*. Chicago, IL: University of Chicago Press.

McCloskey, D. N. (2016). *Bourgeois Equality: How Ideas, not Capitalism or Institutions, Enriched the World*. Chicago, IL: University of Chicago Press.

Mill, J. S. (1859). *On Liberty*. London: Penguin.

Miller, C. (2022). *Chip War: The Fight for the World's Most Critical Technology*. New York: Simon and Schuster.

Mokyr, J. (2002). *The Gifts of Athena: Historical Origins of the Knowledge Economy*. Princeton, NJ: Princeton University Press.

Mokyr, J. (2009). *The Enlightened Economy*. New Haven, CT: Yale University Press.

Mokyr, J. (2017). *A Culture of Growth*. Princeton, NJ: Princeton University Press.

Murray, A., & Whitney, C. (2022). *Tomorrow's Capitalist: My Search for the Soul of Business*. New York: Public Affairs.

Needham, J. (1956). *Science and Civilisation in China*. Cambridge: Cambridge University Press.

Neuhouser, F. (2023). *Diagnosing Social Pathology: Rousseau, Hegel, Marx and Durkheim*. Cambridge: Cambridge University Press.

Nicolis, G., & Prigogine, I. (1989). *Exploring Complexity*. New York: W. H. Freeman.

North, D. C. (1990). *Institutions, Institutional Change and Economic Performance*. Cambridge: Cambridge University Press.

North, D. C. (2005). *Understanding the Process of Economic Change*. Princeton, NJ: Princeton University Press.

North, D. C., Wallis, J. J., Webb, S. B., & Weingast, B. R. (2007). 'Limited access orders in the developing world: a new approach to problems of development'. Policy Research Working Paper No. 4359, World Bank, Washington, DC.

Paterson, S. (2021). *For, By, and From the Party: Defining the Parameters of Dual Circulation*. Research Report. Singapore: The Hinrich Foundation.

Pettis, M. (2022). 'How China trapped itself: the CCP's economic model has left it with only bad choices'. *Foreign Affairs*, October 5.

Pinker, S. (2016). *The Blank Slate: The Modern Denial of Human Nature*. London: Penguin.

Pinker, S. (2018). *Enlightenment Now: The Case for Reason, Science, Humanism, and Progress*. London: Allen Lane.

Pinker, S. (2021). *Rationality: What It Is. Why It Seems Scarce. Why It Matters*. London: Allen Lane.

Polanyi, K. (1944). *The Great Transformation*. Boston, MA: Beacon Press.

Popper, K. (1962). *The Open Society and Its Enemies*, Vol. 2. New York: Harper & Row.

Popper, K. R. (1994). *The Myth of the Framework*. London: Routledge.

Ragin, C. C. (1987). *The Comparative Method: Moving Beyond Qualitative and Quantitative Strategies*. Berkeley: University of California Press.

Reach Immigration (2019). 'Here are the top 10 countries to migrate to' (blog), 3 November. https://reachimmigration.com/en/blog/here-are-top-10-countries-to-migrate-to.

Redding, G. (1990). *The Spirit of Chinese Capitalism*. New York: De Gruyter.

Redding, G. (1995). 'Overseas Chinese networks: understanding the enigma'. *Long Range Planning* 28(1), 61–9.

Redding, G. (2005). 'The thick description and comparison of societal systems of capitalism'. *Journal of International Business Studies* 36, 123–55.

Redding, G. (2021). 'Korean cultural industry: modernity at work in societal progress'. Presentation at World Hallyu Congress. Kellogg College, Oxford.

Redding, G. (2023). 'Societal knowledge quality as catalyst for the competitive productivity of technology: one of a set of several universal processes in trajectories of societal progress'. *International Business Review: Special Issue on the Tech Cold War and IB Research*.

Ridley, M. (1996). *The Origins of Virtue*. New York: Viking.

Rifkin, J. (2009). *The Empathetic Civilization: The Race to Global Consciousness in a World in Crisis*. New York: Penguin.

Sadler, A. L. (1937). *The Maker of Modern Japan: The Life of Tokugawa Ieyasu*. London: Allen & Unwin.

Santacreu, A. M., & Zhu, H. (2018). 'What does China's rise in patents mean? A look at quality versus quantity'. *Economic Synopses*, No. 14, Federal Reserve Bank of St. Louis.

Shambaugh, D. (2013). *China Goes Global: The Partial Power*. Oxford: Oxford University Press.

Sissay, L. (2022). *Dei Miracole: Poems on the Underground*. London: The Poetry Society.

Slack, P. (2015). *The Invention of Improvement: Information and Material Progress in Seventeenth-Century England*. Oxford: Oxford University Press

Smith, A. (1759). *The Theory of Moral Sentiments*. London: A Millar.

Smith, A. (1776). *The Wealth of Nations*. London: Strahan and Cadell.

Smith, E. (2021). *Merchants: The Community That Shaped England's Trade and Empire 1550–1650*. New Haven, CT: Yale University Press.

Solarino, A. M., & Buckley, P. J. (2022). 'Equivalence in international business research: a three-step approach'. *Journal of International Business Studies* 101. https://doi.org/10.1057/s41267-022-00562-2.

Solow, R. (1994). 'Perspectives on growth theory'. *Journal of Economic Perspectives* 8(1), 45–54.

Spence, M. (2011). 'The impact of globalization on income and employment: the downside of integrating markets'. *Foreign Affairs* 90(4), 28–36, 37–41.

Streeck, W. (2012). 'How to study contemporary capitalism'. *European Journal of Sociology* 53(1), 1–28. https://doi.org/10.1017/S000397561200001X.

Subramanian, A., & Felman, J. (2022a). 'India's stifled rise: how the state has stifled growth'. *Foreign Affairs*, 101(1), 139–50.

(2022b). 'Why India can't replace China'. *Foreign Affairs*, December 9.

Tan, Y. (2022). *Disaggregating China Inc.: State Strategies in the Liberal Economic Order*. Ithaca, NY: Cornell University Press.

Teets, J. C. (2013). 'Let many civil societies bloom: the rise of consultative authoritarianism in China'. *The China Quarterly Online*, January 23.

Tuchman, B. W. (1962). *The Guns of August*. London: Penguin.

UNESCO (2021). *UNESCO Science Report: The Race Against Time for Smarter Development*. Paris: UNESCO.

Vasquez, I., MacMahon, F., Murphy, R., & Schneider, G. S. (2021). *The Human Freedom Index 2021*. Washington, DC: Cato Institute.

Wang, Y. (2022). *The Rise and Fall of Imperial China: The Social Origins of State Development*. Princeton, NJ: Princeton University Press.

Weber, M. (1930). *The Protestant Ethic and the Spirit of Capitalism*. London: Unwin.

Welzel, C. (2013). *Freedom Rising*. Cambridge: Cambridge University Press.

Welzel, C., Alexander, A. C., & Klasen, S. (2017). The cool water effect: civilization's turn into human empowerment'. Working Paper, GGL Project, Leuphana University, Germany.

West, G. (2017). *Scale: The Universal Laws of Life and Death in Organisms, Cities, and Companies*. London: Weidenfeld and Nicolson.

Whitley, R. (1999). *Divergent Capitalisms*. Oxford: Oxford University Press.

Whitley R. (2006) 'Understanding differences: the search for the social processes constructing and reproducing variety in science and economic organization'. *Organization Studies* 27(8), 1153–77.

Witt, M. A., de Castro, L. R. K., Amaeshi, K. et al. (2018). 'Mapping the business systems of 61 major economies: a taxonomy and implications for varieties of capitalism and business systems research'. *Socio-Economic Review* 16(1), 5–38.

Witt, M. A., Lewin, A. Y., Liu, P. P., & Gaur, A. (2023). 'Decoupling in international business: evidence, drivers, impact, and implications for IB research', *Journal of World Business*, 58, 101399.

Witt, M. A., & Redding, G. (eds.) (2014) *The Oxford Handbook of Asian Business Systems*. Oxford: Oxford University Press.

Wooldridge, A. (2021). *The Aristocracy of Talent: How Meritocracy Made the Modern World*. London: Allen Lane.

Yamashita, S. H. (1996). 'Confucianism and the Japanese State, 1904–1945'. In W.-M. Tu (ed.), *Confucian Traditions in East Asian Modernity*. Cambridge MA: Harvard University Press, 132–54.

Yuen, S. (2015). 'Friend or foe? The diminishing space of China's civil society'. *China Perspectives* 3, 51–6. https://doi.org/10.4000/chinaperspectives6807.

Youwei (2015). 'The end of reform in China'. *Foreign Affairs*, May–June.

Zitelmann, R. (2019). 'State capitalism'. *Forbes*, 30 September.

# Cambridge Elements ☰

# Reinventing Capitalism

## Arie Y. Lewin
*Duke University, The Fuqua School of Business*

Arie Y. Lewin is Professor Emeritus of Strategy and International Business at Duke University, Fuqua School of Business. He is an Elected Fellow of the Academy of International Businessand a Recipient of the Academy of Management inaugural Joanne Martin Trailblazer Award.Previously, he was Editor-in-Chief of *Management and Organization Review* (2015–2021) and the *Journal of International Business Studies* (2000–2007), founding Editor-in-Chief of *Organization Science* (1989–2007), and Convener of Organization Science Winter Conference(1990–2012). His research centers on studies of organizations' adaptation as co-evolutionarysystems, the emergence of new organizational forms, and adaptive capabilities of innovatingand imitating organizations. His current research focuses on de-globalization anddecoupling, the Fourth Industrial Revolution, and the renewal of capitalism.

## Till Talaulicar
*University of Erfurt, Germany*

Till Talaulicar holds the Chair of Organization and Management at the University of Erfurt where he is also the Dean of the Faculty of Economics, Law and Social Sciences. His main research expertise is in the areas of corporate governance and the responsibilities of the corporate sector in modern societies. Professor Talaulicar is Editor-in-Chief of Corporate Governance: An International Review, Senior Editor of Management and Organization Review and serves on the Editorial Board of Organization Science. Moreover, he has been Founding Member and Chairperson of the Board of the International Corporate Governance Society (2014–2020).

## About the Series

This series seeks to feature explorations about the crisis of legitimacy facing capitalism today, including the increasing income and wealth gap, the decline of the middle class, threats to employment due to globalization and digitalization, undermined trust in institutions, discrimination against minorities, global poverty and pollution. Being grounded in a business and management perspective, the series incorporates contributions from multiple disciplines on the causes of the current crisis and potential solutions to renew capitalism.

Panmure House is the final and only remaining home of Adam Smith, Scottish philosopher and 'Father of modern economics.' Smith occupied the House between 1778 and 1790, during which time he completed the final editions of his master works: The Theory of Moral Sentiments and The Wealth of Nations. Other great luminaries and thinkers of the Scottish Enlightenment visited Smith regularly at the House across this period. Their mission is to provide a world-class twenty-first-century centre for social and economic debate and research, convening in the name of Adam Smith to effect positive change and forge global, future-focussed networks.

## Cambridge Elements ☰

# Reinventing Capitalism

## Elements in the Series

*Taming Corporate Power in the 21st Century*
Gerald F. Davis

*The New Enlightenment: Reshaping Capitalism and the Global Order in the 21st Century*
Edited by Arie Y. Lewin, Greg Linden and David J. Teece

*Reinventing Capitalism in the Digital Age*
Stephen Denning

*From Financialisation to Innovation in UK Big Pharma: AstraZeneca and GlaxoSmithKline*
Öner Tulum, Antonio Andreoni and William Lazonick

*Comparing Capitalisms for an Unknown Future*
Gordon Redding

A full series listing is available at: www.cambridge.org/RECA

Printed in the United States
by Baker & Taylor Publisher Services